enough

Strong Enough • Brave Enough
Loved Enough • Free Enough • I'm Enough
Sheree Wright

First published by Ultimate World Publishing 2025
Copyright © 2025 Sheree Wright

ISBN

Paperback: 978–1–923255–96–8
Ebook: 978–1–923255–97–5

Sheree Wright has asserted her rights under the Copyright, Designs and Patents Act 1988 to be identified as the author of this work. The information in this book is based on the author's experiences and opinions. The publisher specifically disclaims responsibility for any adverse consequences which may result from use of the information contained herein. Permission to use information has been sought by the author. Any breaches will be rectified in further editions of the book.

All rights reserved. No part of this publication may be reproduced, stored in or introduced into a retrieval system, or transmitted in any form, or by any means (electronic, mechanical, photocopying, recording or otherwise) without the prior written permission of the author. Any person who does any unauthorised act in relation to this publication may be liable to criminal prosecution and civil claims for damages. Enquiries should be made through the publisher.

Cover design: Ultimate World Publishing
Layout and typesetting: Ultimate World Publishing
Editor: Carmela Julian Valencia

Ultimate World Publishing
Diamond Creek,
Victoria Australia 3089
www.writeabook.com.au

Testimonials

Sheree Wright's *Enough* is an exceptional blend of honesty, vulnerability and deep insight. With remarkable courage, Sheree takes readers on a profound journey into her eating disorder – unpacking how it began, the factors that fuelled it and the far-reaching impact it had, and has, on her life. Through her reflections, she masterfully pieces together the thoughts, beliefs and emotions that drive such behaviour, helping us better understand not only her story but ourselves and others.

Sheree's weaving together of her personal struggle, with the exploration of her faith, is as educational as it is uplifting. Reading *Enough* gave me a deeper understanding of Sheree's journey but also offered tools and perspectives to reflect on my own sense of self-worth, my relationship with Jesus and how we all seek to feel 'enough'. Sheree's wisdom and gift with words brought me to moments of raw reflection and genuine empowerment. Her story is one of hope, grace and resilience, leaving me deeply moved and unable to put the book down.

Congratulations and thank you, Sheree, for sharing this gift with the world.

Benita Bensch – Author of *The Art of Trying*

Sometimes the people who 'display' themselves so well have a whole world of uncertainty playing out on the inside. They face a struggle no one else can see. They feel trapped and alone. In her book *Enough*, Sheree so bravely shares her struggle and so beautifully shares that we are never alone.

There is Someone who knows us fully. Someone who cares deeply and loves extravagantly and embraces us just as we are. His name is Jesus. He is enough for us. And we are enough for Him, just as we are. He is the One who brings about the deepest healing and wholeness and freedom as we surrender to Him.

Whether you are in a struggle, or know someone who is, this book is for you. May Sheree's raw and brave testimony give you hope and magnify your bravery to step into 'ENOUGH' too.

Petra Cranney

Disclaimer

The content of this book is intended for informational and inspirational purposes only. It is not a substitute for professional medical advice, diagnosis, or treatment. Always seek the advice of your physician or other qualified health providers with any questions you may have regarding a medical condition.

The author shares personal experiences and opinions in this book. These are subjective and may not apply to everyone. Readers are encouraged to consider their own circumstances and consult with professionals as needed.

The information provided in this book is accurate and true to the best of the author's knowledge, but there may be omissions, errors, or mistakes. The author is not liable for any damages or negative consequences from any actions taken by the reader based on the information contained in this book.

If you are experiencing an emergency, crisis, or severe mental health issues, please contact emergency services or a mental health professional immediately.

Dedication

This book is dedicated to anyone who needs reminding that they are enough.

Wrapped up in the word *enough* is the heart line from the depths of history to the heights of eternity, that align us with our true purpose and self.

There is **only** one of us.

In the entire world of millions and billions of people throughout history, there is **one** very **unique** you, and you were placed here in this moment in time for a reason.

My hope is that you grab hold of that reason, or at least take a shaky, courageous step towards finding out what it is and then continue to live passionately on purpose. If nothing else, my hope and prayer is that you know light and life in the darkness we face and that you believe (even if just a little) that you are indeed enough. There is nothing else to add or take away. Right here, right now, in this moment, God

enough

wants to meet you and lead you into His love, accepting you just as you are.

There is no other vice that will fill that void inside your heart. We all have access to exactly what we need. It's just a matter of seeking it out.

Blessings and love beyond measure.

May you walk in your 'enoughness' today and share your gifts with others. The world needs you.

Contents

Testimonials	iii
Disclaimer	v
Dedication	vii
Introduction	1
CHAPTER 1: The Beginning	7
CHAPTER 2: My Imperfect Junk	19
CHAPTER 3: Enough With the Lies	27
CHAPTER 4: It's All Good on the Outside	41
CHAPTER 5: Finding Hope in the Hopelessness	57
CHAPTER 6: I'm So Exhausted From the Fight	73
CHAPTER 7: The Unseen Battle and Warfare	89
CHAPTER 8: You are NOT a Victim	109
CHAPTER 9: The Death of the Thing That Tried to Kill Me and the Love That Set Me Free	123
CHAPTER 10: Confession: The Giant Leap to Healing	135
CHAPTER 11: What If It's Not About Me?	145
CHAPTER 12: Are You Willing to Fight?	159
CHAPTER 13: When the Mountain Doesn't Move	173
Afterword	177
About The Author	179
Speaker Bio	181
Acknowledgements	183

Introduction

Google search about 1,990,000 results (0.39 seconds) May 10, 2018

Bulimia (boo–LEE–me–uh) nervosa, commonly called **bulimia**, is a serious, potentially life–threatening eating disorder. People with **bulimia** may secretly binge – eating large amounts of food with a loss of control over the eating – and then purge, trying to get rid of the extra calories in an unhealthy way.

Symptoms: Binge eating

bulimia

noun

an emotional disorder characterised by a distorted body image and an obsessive desire to lose weight, in which bouts of extreme overeating are followed by fasting or self–induced vomiting or purging.

enough

Binge eating involves two key features:

Eating a very large amount of food within a relatively short period of time (e.g. within two hours)

Feeling a sense of loss of control while eating (e.g. feeling unable to stop yourself from eating)

A person with bulimia nervosa can become lost in a dangerous cycle of out of control eating and attempts to compensate, which can lead to feelings of shame, guilt and disgust. These behaviours can become more compulsive and uncontrollable over time and lead to an obsession with food, thoughts about eating (or not eating), weight loss, dieting and body image.

These behaviours are often concealed, and people with bulimia can go to great lengths to keep their eating and exercise habits secret. As a result, bulimia can often go undetected for long periods of time.

Many people with bulimia nervosa experience weight fluctuations and do not lose weight; they can remain in the normal weight range, be slightly underweight, or may even gain weight.

The snippet above is a brief overview that pretty much summarises a glimpse of what I was experiencing. I do not like to offer any links or recommendations to any specific help centres or programs; there are many resources and organisations that are available for that worldwide. To find out more about the warning signs, I encourage you to engage in your own research.

Introduction

> *If you or someone you love is at risk of an eating disorder, start a conversation in love. The only way out is to first recognise and shine a light into their darkness. If you would like to connect with me and a community of love overflowing individuals – I invite you to my website, www.shereewrightauthor.com.au, where you can access a downloadable resource and find a link to my calendar to book a complimentary 20-minute connection call.*

I always anticipated this book would be an account of victory over my eating disorder. Yet, the goalpost for completing it (or even starting it) kept moving forward as I faced the challenges of my disorder, year after year, season after season. Maybe I will never fully recover or heal from this thing. Maybe this is my story – unfolding, continually changing and moving. Perhaps there's wisdom to be found here.

I've concluded that this needs to be a story told in the midst of my journey. Healed and walking free or not, it needs to be shared.

This book is a revelation moment that 'grace is sufficient'. Grace is essential. This is me living out and walking out my faith journey to discover that, in fact, the God I serve is enough and anything I desire in this world outside of His love would never satisfy. It is better to be fully content, confident and living my fullest life – even with the imperfect junk I carry.

Everyone has some kind of imperfect junk. That's life. No one is immune from challenges, whether they be external trials or internal battles. Everyone has something they struggle with at some stage in their life or throughout their whole life.

enough

For me, it's been food.

People from the outside looking in might see my size 8–10 body and smiling happy face and think I've got it all together.

I **do not** have it all together.

Let's be truthful here: I am not perfect. I do not have all the self-control and delightful thinking you perceive or desire.

Very far from it. I'm a mess, and this story is the exposure of my mess and my continual discovery that I am enough. It's the repeated reassurance that it's OK. And if it doesn't seem that way right now, it will be. It will be OK.

If this helps just one person question or explore their relationship with God and brings them to a deeper understanding of their purpose and mission in life, then my life and my story will have an eternal impact. That outcome is greater than any worldly success or accolades I may receive for writing good content.

My prayer is that you open your heart and mind to the possibilities for you, wherever you are on your journey.

Before writing my story, I expected to have some kind of healing strategy and victory to share with you. I thought I would delve deeply into how I overcame my struggles, what I did in the midst of my inner storm to find the peace I was searching for. I expected to outline how you could apply these strategies to your struggle or storm and step into living the life of your dreams. Turns out I don't have that strategy to share with you. Sounds amazing though, doesn't it?

Introduction

My freedom formula is Jesus. He has no formula; it is a walk of faith and surrender bound by love. To walk by faith is to activate a deep belief and conviction that you know it will be OK. To trust someone is to hold on to the hope that what they promise they can do for you, they will do – even if you can't see it yet.

It doesn't look like 'start with prayer, then journal and colour your feelings, look up some scriptures and positive affirmations, then stare at yourself in the mirror and try to believe you are worth loving'. I've tried all that, and it didn't work for me.

I completely respect everyone else's journey, so please don't think this is some kind of 'convert you to become a follower of Jesus' sales funnel. It's not that at all. This is **my** journey, and I'm so grateful you are here.

This is my story and my experience of discovering a personal relationship with Christ Jesus that ultimately led me to find true freedom from the thing that was destroying my soul – an inner battle with food. Eating disorder. Mental health issues. Bulimia. Whatever you want to label it as, this is my 'no formula' journey to freedom. I trust that by sharing it, someone, somewhere in the world will find hope. Even if it's just a glimmer; it can be all you need to keep going.

My no-formula strategy looks like this:

- ♥ 'Trust and follow me'
- ♥ 'Surrender your will to my will, and I will overflow love into your life and through your life, reaching an amount that no one can measure.'

enough

These are not scriptures or biblical quotes; these are whispers I heard in my soul.

Jesus is a Good Shepherd – and I know people don't like to say we should be as dumb as sheep and follow the leader around, but a shepherd protects, takes care of the whole being and leads the sheep to safety. If you're in an unsafe place and need a hand to hold, please let me encourage you with these words and the story that follows.

I hope you find freedom, because life is too short to be living in torment and helplessness. Life is too short to remain lost.

It's time to come home. Let's go.

CHAPTER 1

The Beginning

I'm pretty sure I had a close-to-normal upbringing – two parents (a mum and a dad), two older brothers, a small-town lifestyle, family holidays and adventures, a safe home, close friends, no trauma or significant illness. Sounds pretty ordinary to me. So, how or why would someone like me develop a severe eating disorder at 15 years of age? What is the underlying root cause that triggers this kind of mental, physical and emotional struggle?

I was born into a hardworking family in Crookwell, NSW in 1984. I joined two older brothers, completing our family of five (Brett was almost 8 years old, and Shane just 16 months old). My dad was a shearer, and my mum the lady of all trades.

enough

As well as being there for us a lot of the time, Mum worked and volunteered in many fields (shearers' cook, bus driver, tuckshop lady, cleaner, swimming pool attendant and shop assistant, to name a few) throughout our childhood. Dad worked away a lot. Brett was at primary school. Shane and I spent our days with Mum, following her busy schedule.

When I was almost 6, we moved to Goolgowi, NSW, a small country town around 400 kilometres away from our hometown, to be closer to Dad's workplaces. I was starting kindergarten in a class of 15 children within a school of 85 children in total. Friendships were formed immediately. Everyone had a place. There was no social hierarchy because we all existed together and needed each other. The policeman's family, the publican, the kindergarten teacher – they all had something in common, and there was always a community event of some kind to bring us together.

My life was blessed. We shared so many moments of a 'typical', 'ordinary' or 'average' Australian family living in a small country town – a community blend of rural farming families and local teachers, council workers, feedlot workers and shop owners. There wasn't a lot to do or see in terms of tourist attractions or entertainment, but we had a very good life.

Our holidays were spent camping out at the sheds wherever Dad was shearing. We would pack up our 'farm clothes' and go along with Mum to join Dad in the caravan. Our new home and playground were the shearing shed, yards and quarters. Our fun was comprised of helping Mum in the kitchen with 1,000 smokos, climbing wool bales, getting in the way, tackling sheep, sliding down the sheep shoot and climbing gates, yards, trees – anything that we could get dirty on. Our days were

The Beginning

long and fulfilled. Hearing banter between the shearers and support staff, rouseabouts, wool pressers and farmers gave us a sense of extended family gatherings that we were missing out on, being so far away from our cousins and family.

In 1997, I entered Griffith High School in our main town, 50 kilometres away. Coming from a small town and small school to a massive high school was a bit of a culture shock to my social nervous system. Most of my closest friends went to boarding schools, while only three of us from Goolgowi Primary went to Griffith High School. Apart from two girls, I knew only one other girl entering a grade of around 180 students.

Shane was a year above me and had quite a strong opinion of how incredibly different high school would be. Compared to our protected small-school bubble of 10 girls and one boy graduating, the shock of entering large classes was real. It seemed like everyone already had their friend groups established from primary school. They did life together. They had already celebrated each other's birthdays and had a clique going on that we, small-town kids, didn't really understand. Everyone was in 'groups', like there was an unwritten application system they all went through to get allocated to a team.

I was split into a different class from the other two girls coming from Goolgowi and found myself shuffling through Year 7, just trying to figure out where I fit. I didn't play any sports – we were too far out of town, and with Mum and Dad committed to the local General Store they had purchased in 1995, most of my spare time was spent playing shopkeeper with them. Serving customers, packing shelves, cleaning and keeping cold drinks at the front of the fridge were my after-school activities. I gained

enough

so much knowledge and a solid work ethic from this period in my life. There was always something that needed doing.

Going on a holiday together as a family was a big deal because Mum and Dad had to orchestrate replacements for themselves in the shop and ensure things kept running while they were gone. It was very rare to get away or do weekend activities because of the logistics involved, so work was life. We could be in the shop anywhere from 6 am to 8.30 pm. Shane and I would catch the school bus at 7.30 am and arrive home at 5 pm.

I never really had an urge or desire to play sports or be involved in any extracurricular activities. I never had a team–sport spirit. Solo has been the default for me. That way I can accomplish what I need to, and if I don't I'm not letting anyone else down. This created a comfort zone that led me to fly solo on most things.

During high school, I mastered the skill of procrastination and putting things off until the very last minute (or even past their due date) – which I could never understand, but I functioned that way. Most of the time, I avoided doing the thing until I had no choice. I would spend those last few hours of the night before something was due, or even on the morning of the due date, and pull a sickie to produce my best work and perfect every little detail. It worked. I did what I needed to and accomplished pretty good marks in most of my subjects.

My favourite subject was math; I was naturally good at it. It's easy and natural for me to crunch numbers. Like I said earlier, I am a detailed person. I like attention to detail and having a balanced equation. I didn't favour English at all. It left too many open options for my work to be critiqued. I never read a book that was assigned in class. If we had to write an essay

The Beginning

about a book, I would participate in the in-class reading and then, if I could, watch the movie and summarise from there.

I breezed through a lot in my high school years on the whim of winging it and just fluking many half-hearted attempts at reaching for good grades. Somehow, I landed with good grades, which created a perception that I was a 'good girl', that I was studious. I was not.

I had a few favourite teachers and generally got along pretty well in class. I had a beautiful group of friends by Year 8, and we never really made a fuss in class. We were never disruptive or disrespectful to the teachers. OK, maybe there were one or two relief teachers we all hammered pretty hard, but it was a rare occasion, and we never pushed beyond the typical teenage limits. Nothing ever warranted a report or visit to the Principal.

We were the group of girls that were 'in the middle' of the pack. We weren't the popular girls who went to parties on the weekend, and we weren't the shy and keep-to-yourself girls. We were in the middle – all getting along, doing our work, not too interested in the distraction of boys.

Retracing where my bulimia began, there was a significant moment in Grade 10 science that I remember. What I've discovered since unpacking that moment has been so critical to understanding the depths of my mental struggle, journey of destruction and the path to healing that lay ahead.

We're in the science lab classroom, beginning the lesson just after lunch. I hate science. I'm not sure if it's the teacher and the way they deliver the content or if it just clashes with my I-can't-be-bothered-with-this-stuff-right-now teenage attitude. Either

way, I wasn't interested and had this overwhelming feeling that I didn't want to be there. Maybe something was due, and I didn't have it ready to hand in (not unusual for me). Maybe there was a topic test or something uncomfortable or difficult I was expected to complete. Whatever it was, I wanted out.

Dramatically, I stood from my chair, said I needed to go to the bathroom quickly and rushed out. I paced out of the corridor, down the wide concrete stairs surrounded by concrete walls, through the quadrangle, across to the toilet block. I could smell cigarettes. Someone was sneaking a ciggy, like they do before going back to class because they know there are no teachers around. I hoped they wouldn't see or hear me.

I entered the girl's toilet block, chose a cubicle and latched the door behind me in a desperate need to have something come from this. I wasn't actually sick, but I was willing myself sick. Who runs from class, rushing to get to a toilet in anticipation of being sick and then doesn't get sick?! That wouldn't be good to have to explain.

I bent over, lifted the seat, allowed the blood to rush to my head, then pressed on my stomach hard enough until nausea washed over me. Then came lunch, a bulk exit of whatever bread roll I had eaten just an hour or so before. My eyes watered, my head pounded. It felt so gross, but it felt good in comparison to what I felt about myself. Reflecting back, my subconscious beliefs and insecurities were running this show, and it was not in my best interest. Getting rid of all the food that day had me feeling accomplished, like I had a reason to be sick. It doesn't feel good to vomit, but it validated my leaving the science lab and getting out of class.

The Beginning

I shuffled back to class, trying to remain looking sick, enough for people to know it was legit but not too much that I would have to explain myself. If someone had asked and really shown concern, I don't think I could have answered. I didn't know what was wrong. No, actually, I knew there was **nothing** wrong but didn't know why I **wanted** something to be wrong.

It's so confusing to comprehend; all I can put it down to now, as I dive deep into understanding, is that self-pity was a way to pacify myself from the reality that I didn't feel good enough. If I wasn't good enough and the reason was out of my control, I was a victim. Being a victim meant I would get overcompensated with attention that showed me people cared – or at least made me feel like they had to care – when the noise in my head was stirring with the argument that nobody cares. The truth is I didn't care. Others cared about me. But I didn't.

That was the very beginning, the first ever purge incident. It was birthed from a place of disgust, wanting to have an excuse not to face the thing I needed to do (or be) in class. From that moment, there were times at home when I would play a similar scenario (but not the dramatic exit) after dinner. I knew it was possible to simply lean over the toilet bowl long enough to push hard on my stomach and allow the recently consumed meal to exit my body.

To view that scenario from my current position of wife and mother – imagining that 15-year-old alone, afraid, unsure and so awfully disgusted at herself for not being good enough, to see that she punishes herself so much in secret and in desperation – breaks my heart. I want to bust through that bathroom door, hold a hand on her back, pull her hair from her face, look into her teary, bloodshot eyes and say, 'Sweetheart, it's not worth

enough

it. You can stop now. You can walk away from this and learn from what is actually going on. You have so much to offer the world. You are gifted, talented, beautiful, wise and amazing at being you. Please don't squash that. Don't throw that away. Please don't feel like you need to make yourself feel this way in order to receive pity or love. **You are loved** far beyond measure, and you are **capable** of far more than you know.

Stand up tall, gorgeous one. Wash your face. Put your shoulders back and stare into those eyes and declare, "Sheree, I love you, I really, really love you." Whatever you are feeling right now is OK. We can get through this. We are going to shine a light on the lies and eliminate the negative, destructive labels you are holding on yourself right now. They are **not** who you were created to be. I want **all** of you to thrive and shine in the world for the purposes planted deep within your heart.

Please accept my love; let me love you. Know that you are worthy of being loved, and no matter what happens or whatever comes your way, you will be OK. There is no need to retreat and run and numb yourself from the pain. Sometimes pain and discomfort are the process of growth. You were born to grow. Please don't squash that growth now. There is so much joy and delight to be had in your life. Experiencing these emotions is all part of the human experience.

Sheree, I love you. I want the best for you. You are amazing. You can do hard things. Let's do this gently and kindly and peacefully – not in war with yourself. Sheree, I love you.'

I would wrap my arms around her and hold on tight until she **feels** all of that. Until the wholeness of her being was completely surrendered and trusting that this was **truth**.

The Beginning

As this 'sickness' unravelled, I occasionally used it to pull pity from my parents. I would share that I've been sick, hiding the fact that I secretly was bringing it on myself, and they would express concern.

'We need to get a doctor's appointment to find out what's going on. You shouldn't still be throwing up this many times if it was a bug or something causing it,' Mum said one day.

So, off we went to the doctor's. Sitting in the waiting room, awkwardly observing everyone, I was wondering if **any** of them could tell what was happening to me – just a self-conscious observation that maybe someone knew more than I did, because deep down I had no idea and was hoping the doctors could give it a name so that I could again validate my actions. I kind of felt it wasn't in my head, but then I did think extremely hard about feeling so terrible to become sick, so I was willing it but wanted there to be something wrong.

We were called into the doctor's office. The doctor asked some questions, which Mum answered and looked at me to agree. I didn't have a lot to say, and I was banking on the information Mum was giving them because I didn't really give her the whole picture of what was going on. I didn't know why I **wanted** to be sick and bring myself to throw up, but I knew I did it not because of an obvious physical ailment. I knew they weren't going to find anything – but I wanted them to.

After going through a recall of some of the things I had been eating, we were given some dietary restrictions – cut back the caffeine (so no iced coffee in the morning when I get off the bus before school), no more chocolate after lunch, limit the amount of high fatty foods and go easy on the things that

enough

place strain on my digestive system. These limitations were OK with me. I could easily control my intake and not be too put out by them. Mum had always been on some kind of fad diet – Weight Watchers, Jenny Craig or something where she had to journal and record all of the foods she ate at what times. I could be just like Mum, then – no more iced coffee, no chocolate after lunch, limit the high fatty foods, keep a record. Easy.

However, my self-induced vomits continued and became more frequent. I was losing weight – although that was not the goal – and it felt like there was now some physical evidence that would show people I was actually sick and wasn't making it up. Being able to hide the truth felt powerful. No one needed to know what was leading to each purge.

I became a little stand-offish with food because if I didn't eat, then I wouldn't have to throw up. Cutting back what I ate made more sense – I could be secretly starving, and each hunger pain was a reminder that I was sick and there was something wrong. I had no idea at the time that emotions and chemical imbalances and dopamine hits and all the things I know now were driving all of this.

We made a visit back to the doctor's to explain that the food restrictions didn't cure anything. The doctor resolved that it must be more of a mental battle this time, and because I confirmed I was withholding from eating a lot, their assumption was that I was having issues with body image and possibly going down the eating disorder path.

I assured my parents I wasn't – and that was the truth. I wasn't withholding from the food because I was concerned about my

The Beginning

weight at all. It had nothing to do with body image, but I had no idea it was rooted in self-image and self-talk and self-worth. I never ever put these things together. I understood that people with eating disorders were concerned about how they looked. My issue was a fight with feelings.

'Here are some leaflets about eating disorders and where to get help,' the doctor handed Mum some pamphlets.

What a joke, I thought. It's not an eating disorder. It's not in my head. I have no issues with my body.

We went back home and discussed what might be going on in my mind to cause this vomiting to happen. I read the information about the help services for eating disorders and immediately ruled out that it would help me.

I didn't fit the criteria at all.

CHAPTER 2

My Imperfect Junk

In April of 2000, I met a boy – an 18-year-old boy with a WB ute, working on the council to help his aunty who was recovering from thyroid cancer. He was super cute. He had all the country looks a 15-year-old small-town girl could wish for – and he wasn't a local, so that was even better! I can brag on how amazing he was then because he ended up becoming my husband and is still pretty brag-worthy, given what we've been through.

Chris was working on the parks and gardens, helping his Aunty Helen with her workload as she recovered from her thyroid cancer treatment. Aunty Helen and Chris were regular visitors at the shop that Mum and Dad owned. During their morning visits for their daily smoko run, Aunty Helen had regular chats with my mum and dad about Chris being a good

enough

possibility of a boyfriend for me. I was not looking, and Mum and Dad (I hope) were not looking to sell me off, but the idea blossomed into the question that Chris asked – 'Can Sheree come with me when I walk my dogs in the afternoon?'. Along with Mum, Dad and Helen playing set-ups, Helen's 12-year-old daughter Jodie also played a part and would phone me to say that Chris really, really wanted me to go with him when he walked the dogs.

I **did not** know how to hang out with boys. I was the good girl at school. What would I say? What do I wear? How do I act? Ugh, I'm such a nerd. He's waaaay too good (and good-looking) for me. But what do I have to lose? At least he's not a boy from school. They're all townie-like – hip hop and stuff. I liked the loud ute, cowboy hat and the all-round mystery of dating an 18-year-old – in Year 10! I'm 15; as if I would ever find anyone this good at school. All the good ones will be taken by the time I'm ready to date.

So, sure, let's go on a date!

The confidence I received from being **that** girl getting picked up by the cowboy in the WB Ute from the school bus stop on a rainy day made me feel like one of the cool girls without even needing to be in the cool girl crowd. I was in a league of my own.

Although, I really didn't feel that special.

Around the time of meeting Chris, our dear Poppy Rigg, Mum's dad, passed away. This was the first close family member I had ever lost, and it was so hard. We didn't see our grandparents often, being located so far away, but when we did go and visit them, we had good quality time and created amazing memories that all grandchildren treasure. Poppy was the gentle and kind, soft, old man who would take his hearing aid out so he didn't have to listen to Nana nagging or waffling. He would watch Sale of the Century and Wheel of Fortune on full bore volume, his hearing aid turned down. We got to play amongst the living room clutter and drown in the noise with him away from Nana – also nagging and waffling at us.

I was so sad to say goodbye to Poppy, but meeting Chris was perfect timing, as I could divert my attention away from the big questions of life. Meeting Chris meant I could focus on new love and romance without a care in the world for any other serious issue.

I had no idea what my mum was feeling; I don't remember emotions being expressed in any significant way. I certainly didn't comfort her or consider what it even means to suddenly lose a dad. He was not sick. He didn't have an accident. It was just a sudden, middle-of-the-night heart attack.

It must have been horrible for Mum, but my focus was Chris – a real country boy with a job and a ute and damn good looks. Can you blame me at 15, truly self-centred and self-consumed?

While my friendship and relationship with Chris deepened, my sickness sort of crept in. While I had Chris as a new distraction from school and feeling like I didn't fully belong or fit in, my sickness did consume me when I was alone. When no one was around, I was a mess – torment in my head, cravings taking over me, urge to eat and eat and eat all sorts of extravagant things and then throw up before Mum and Dad were finished

enough

in the shop and we would have dinner as a family. I would still secretly throw up after dinner, feeling accomplished that I could suffer in silence and mask the real pain I was feeling in regard to my unworthiness. Whenever I felt like I was not enough, I could affirm that belief with the guilt and shame layering from how often I was throwing up and hiding from my loved ones.

We already tried to solve this, I thought, *and according to everyone around me, it's not as big an issue anymore. I have dug myself too deep now to open up and be honest. I need to keep it hidden and out of sight, otherwise I'll need to own up to all of the lies and sneaking and hiding I've been doing.*

There was a point throughout Year 10 when Mum and I looked at the possibility of me heading off to boarding school at Orange to complete Years 11 and 12. I applied for and received a half scholarship to attend, so it was looking doable.

Going away meant that I would not have to spend as much time travelling on the bus every day and it would offer me more opportunities to advance my education. I didn't particularly value my education that much and wasn't highly driven. The results I had achieved so far were a reflection of natural talent, not backed by hard work or striving. I bluffed my way to this point and mastered the art of procrastination on deadlines like a professional. School was extremely stressful because of this procrastinating approach. I didn't cope with the internal pressure I was placing on myself (mostly to be perfect and get things perfect and just be highly achieving all the time), but no one knew. I had also mastered the art of gracefully cruising along like a duck on water, while underneath my little duck legs were paddling like mad, trying to stay afloat.

My Imperfect Junk

I continued breezing my way throughout the end of my school certificate exams. I received an early exit pass to leave school straight after the Year 10 exams and start a full-time job. Coincidentally, a family that I had been babysitting for on the usual Friday night parental outing since I was 12 years old wanted a full-time nanny to be with their four children during the day while they worked onsite at their family-owned grain storage complex. This was perfect! I was playing mum and being boss lady plus fun lady with three little kids while the oldest one went off to school.

My nanny job was awesome. I've always said it was the best degree in parenting I've ever done, and I owe a lot of my strategy and wisdom now to learning from those experiences and discovering what works and what doesn't with different ages and stages of kids. Being a 16-year-old household manager of four children under 7 years old is a pretty extreme ask if I look at 16-year-olds today, but it matured me beyond my years and I began a whole level of respect for the work that parents do in shaping the life of another human being (or several, in this case).

Obviously, Mum and I decided against the Orange scholarship because I had become so invested in Chris and I that I couldn't imagine leaving him to be away at school. We both thought that would be the dying days of our relationship, and neither of us wanted that. Plus, my lack of enthusiasm for school backed me pretty surely that getting into the workforce was a much better idea.

Most of my friends stayed on. I still had amazing connections with my primary friends who had been away at boarding school this whole time. And then there was the group of girls

enough

with whom I survived Years 8 through 10, who dedicated themselves to finishing Grade 12. I was the only one in our friend group who had a boyfriend, and I felt myself shifting away again from feeling like I fit in.

Work was a good distraction from this, and I found that I wasn't out of control with my eating as much as I seemed to be getting home from school every day and repeating habitual behaviours. Handling the kids meant I was investing in them and taking the focus off myself.

I did find myself on occasions, though, where I would binge and find a way to gourmandise and secretly get rid of everything I ate and all of the evidence – packets of biscuits and chips, ice cream, chocolate (even chocolate chips or cooking chocolate), cake batter, icing and anything I could get my hands on that seemed easy to throw up and provided the specific craving holeshot I needed. I would strategically dispose of all the packaging or wrapping so that no one would have any idea.

I found myself flushing the toilet several times to get rid of the smell and debris of leftover layers of oil, fat and anything that didn't sink first time around. Placing the kids in front of the TV for this exercise was perfect while I prepared their dinner and binged on the side.

In February 2001, Chris asked me if I wanted to get engaged. I was almost 17; it was a definite yes. We co-purchased with my mum and dad, a house just down the road, gathered our household furniture and settled in, ready to start out a new life together. I bought my first car, paying cash from all the babysitting and shop work I had done.

My Imperfect Junk

My nannying job quickly turned into a full-time office job, as the family I worked for expanded their business and needed someone to help with their bookwork. They were pretty keen on my natural maths ability and attention to detail, so they offered to put me on as a trainee to do business administration. It was easier to get another nanny to replace me than it was to find willing and available office staff. All of the local talents were already consumed within the council office, school and feedlot out of town.

The office was another swaying distraction from my chance to binge all day every day. Still, there were plenty of times when I had the office to myself. If caught off guard in my emotions, I would spend valuable work time snacking away at my desk to a point of overindulgence. This would lead me, once again, to sneak off to the toilets, unload the contents of my stomach, and then guzzle water, fizzy drink, and more water for a final washout or emptying of my stomach and start a clean slate all over again.

I was **not** well. I don't even know how I functioned. Once I encountered a strong enough craving, I couldn't concentrate until I satisfied it. My brain capacity had been so impaired from the malnourishment, and dehydration had been my constant state. I just went into survival mode.

Now I can't even imagine the level of torment I put my organs through, let alone my mental and emotional state. I marvel at the way our bodies operate and am so surprised at how much we take for granted. There was such a ping-pong, yo-yo going on that I would have displayed all sorts of crazy deficiencies and malfunctions if anyone were to run me under the medical microscope. No one did that, though. I was an adult making

my own choices, running my own agenda. Mum had little input in anything I was doing, and Chris was so oblivious, I guess, being in love with me but didn't even know all that was going on because I hid it so damn well!

I was carrying so much guilt and shame and regret after every single binge. **Every** binge. That would be several times a day. I would binge and purge multiple times a day and be completely fried by the end of the day. I couldn't escape myself. If I thought the toilet had taken too much of a pounding, I would vomit into a container, then place it into the bin and send it out to the large Sulo bins out the back, along with all of the food packaging and rubbish I was trying to hide. No one was going to look in the bins.

My neck hurt constantly, strained by the convulsions. My stomach burned with acid damage. My breath disgusting, I would still smoke cigarettes and chew gum like a true teenage rebel. I would go to bed, mentally exhausted from the fight – sometimes trying so hard to resist the temptations and then condemning myself that I couldn't and wasn't strong enough and that my willpower was rubbish. Self-hate, disgust and shame grew bigger and bigger, and the bingeing became more frequent and more intense.

CHAPTER 3

Enough With the Lies

As a 17-year-old with a 20-year-old fiancé, it was really hard to distinguish between truth and lies about your self-worth or even simply acknowledge that you have a level of value and worth. I would never have said out loud that I was unworthy or unlovable, but my actions and my default habits were speaking louder than my conscious thinking. So, I battled (unknowingly) with this inner rage over my worth and value. I battled with food – physically and mentally. I fought daily, hourly, moment by moment. Not a day went by that I didn't abuse myself with what I consumed and how I felt about it. I didn't want to deal with the aftermath that digesting the food would have on my body, so throwing up seemed like the easiest out. I would repeat the cycle of throwing up to get rid of all the junk (and the effects it would have on my body) to begin a clean slate.

enough

Binge followed by the guzzling of water.

Empty the stomach (to the point of nothing left).

Eyes watering, head thumping, chest hurting.

Guilt and shame rising.

A thorough rinse of the mouth or brush of my teeth and replenishing with water so I wasn't left completely malnourished **and** dehydrated.

Clean slate.

Plaster on the next smile and carry on.

Here I go again, ready to face the world. My feelings (whatever they were) were gone and forgotten. I could continue in my little bubble of perfection and carry on like my life is perfect and I have no struggles at all.

I would not treat a friend the way I treated myself. And I certainly wouldn't stay friends with someone who treated me that way. **But** when it's me, and I'm stuck with me, I can't get away from me. It's hard to recognise that my actions were expressing pure hatred towards myself and causing so much suffering for deeply believing these lies:

- No one will like me.
- I'm not good enough.
- I'm not as cool as them.
- I don't have anything worth contributing to the group.

- If only they knew who I really was, they would think differently about me.
- I've made too many mistakes.
- I can't undo the mess I've made so far.
- I'm no good.
- I always stuff it up.

All of these things, completely oblivious to me at the time but later realised, were the poisonous roots causing the horrible fruit in my life. That 'fruit' was uncontrollable bingeing and purging in secret, when no one was around. No one knew, no one would ever know. It was the one thing I thought I **could** control to help deal with all the other things I thought I couldn't control, like this feeling of unworthiness. The inner critic and self-talk that constantly put me down was relentless. I could not escape these thoughts.

These bursts of overeating were linked to my feelings. The fact that I never recognised my feelings and never allowed them to surface and do anything about them kept me in a dangerous trap. I simply suppressed any emotions I couldn't deal with and medicated with food, like a drug addict needing another hit.

My negative self-talk and inner critic were not a belief system formed by other people putting me down. I was not bullied; I had loving family and friends surrounding me all through my life. The fact that the noise inside my head was so mean and so nasty – I couldn't share that with anyone because they believed differently about me. But it was my truth, and nothing that anyone could have said or done to convince me otherwise would have made a difference (or so I thought), so I kept quiet. The thoughts I had were all I knew, and since I didn't express

enough

them, I gave no one the opportunity to correct me or redirect me in any way.

I didn't think we could change the internal blueprint. Convinced it's part of our personality or in our genes, I thought we were born and wired a certain way, and that's how it stays. I later discovered this is called a **fixed mindset**. Little did I know that I could completely rewire my internal dialogue to line up with actual truth – a **growth mindset** – and that would set me free to be me. All of me. Nothing hidden. No guilt. No shame. No more hiding. We all have this opportunity if we are honest and call out the lies for what they are.

My friends were amazing. Some knew but didn't really say anything. They would defend me when someone made a comment that I needed to have a good hamburger because I looked so sick and drawn and too thin. But, they didn't understand why I struggled. I didn't even understand why I struggled. I think this is why I was so resistant to getting help – I didn't expect anyone else to understand since I didn't even understand myself.

I couldn't have explained what was going on if anyone were to ask me.

No one asked me.

Chris loved me, all of me. There was never any pressure or expectations from him to be a certain way or look or dress any particular way. He just loved me.

But I hated me.

Enough With the Lies

I hated myself for the distance I was creating in our relationship – hiding things and keeping secrets around food and bingeing and throwing up. I hated myself because of the resistance I held up to prevent him from coming closer and loving me even deeper. I hated myself for not getting it together. I hated myself for failing again and again and again. False starts and failed finishes over and over again – a pattern so woven into my being that it seemed impossible to unravel now.

This really saddens me to reflect on the pitifulness of that scenario. My husband and I have two daughters who are currently 13 and 9 years old when this book is printed. If I ever found out they were feeling and thinking about themselves in **that** way – with such low self-esteem and low value and worth – it would break the strings of my heart. I want **no one** to feel that way about themselves and treat themselves in such a way, so much that I want a fountain of **love** to pour out of me into everyone I meet so that they can taste and know the reality of real love and hope – for a brighter future. Not a life in the pit, not bound by lies.

I want everyone, young girls especially, to realise the truth and power of their purpose and destiny in this life so that no one would wander around that mountain as many times as I did, cause as much pain and destruction and waste as many wonderful years as I did.

I want, more than anything, to go back and change what I did wrong, but I know that can't happen. So, instead, I will do the next right thing and share my experience to help someone else. I want you to know that you are loved and valued, and you get to walk in that love and value in order to have an abundant life.

enough

During our time at Goolgowi, Chris and I had a pretty fun life. We had a group of friends with whom Chris connected through joining the local football team, and we would socialise as much as the football calendar required. We spent most nights at the pub or club; Wednesday, Thursday and Friday night raffles; Saturday afternoon into the night; Sunday football extending through the night; then it's back to work on Monday. My payday was weekly on a Monday, so it was pretty fabulous to me that when we had spent way too much on alcohol and cigarettes, my bank account was replenished and we could start the week fresh – a lot like the cycle of my eating patterns, always aiming for that clean, fresh start to begin perfect again.

By this time, I had looked into some of the support available around eating disorders. I knew this had escalated far beyond forcing myself to throw up in avoidance of facing my feelings. This was now an obsession, and it consumed all of my life. My body was deteriorating and constantly operating in survival mode. My mental health was a mess, but I didn't know any different, so I just continued in the spirals and uncertainty. My soul flame was slowly dying out, and I had no idea how to spark it back up again.

The help services and material all still pointed to one thing – eating disorders are a result of body image delusion and only the really severe, sick and weak ones go to clinics or hospitals for treatment.

The stories I read were not relatable to my situation at all, so again I disregarded that I could be helped and resolved that it was still up to me. The only person who could help me was me.

Yet, I failed to help myself over and over again.

I proved that I was not faithful at sticking with my word, because this thing was stronger than I was, and I was feeling weaker than ever.

I read stories of women and girls who feared food, debilitated by the pain of having to eat and afraid of what the food would do to their bodies. I didn't fear food, I craved food. Food was my drug. I loved food. I wanted food all the time, but I didn't want to face the physical consequences of being an overeater.

I didn't pay any attention to the science of what was happening in my body as I carried out a binge. I have to say: Knowledge is power. If we arm ourselves with enough knowledge that drives our actions, it's like a superpower. The journey I have been on since looking at how the mind works and how our brain and bodies work **and** how our feelings and emotions tie into that – it's incredibly scientific and incredibly equipping to know just how amazing we are and how we were created to function optimally!

My oblivion and ignorance were keeping me stuck. Pride was keeping me stuck.

There were days when, after work, I didn't particularly want to go with Chris to hang out with friends and socialise, so I would isolate myself to embark on a binge. Alone, but not liking my own company, it was the only way to escape me. A binge often started with something sweet, like chocolate or any high-sugar indulgence I could get my hands on. My physical being was looking for an instant dopamine hit. My emotional being wanted to escape and numb uncertain feelings. My spiritual being was lost and afraid, unaware of my true purpose, unaware of my true value.

enough

Chris and I lived in our first home for about a year before moving to Carrathool, the small town where Chris grew up. His parents owned a house they didn't use, as they were living on a farm, so we moved in, rented out our Goolgowi house, and I started working at the Carrathool Pub as a Business Administration Trainee.

These years were also fun and free – a lot of young people worked in the area at the time, and we spent many late Friday nights partying at the pub and down the river. Often, when I was around people, I was completely fine. I didn't have any social anxiety or insecurities that showed on the outside. My illness became a deep, dark secret I couldn't let anyone know about because:

1. I couldn't explain it and didn't know what was going on, and
2. they would think I was crazy (I actually was!)

This reality drove home that I could not dare share with anyone because being deemed crazy would cost me everything. I had a good, secure job, we paid our bills on time and enjoyed our youthful luxuries, I seemed like a normal young woman living life with her fiancé – no worries in the world.

But I did worry. I worried if I would ever be able to stop, because it seemed to me that the longer it went on, the harder I fell each time and the heavier the weight was to bear as I tried to 'get back up' again.

I cannot describe the level of guilt and shame. I look back now and think if I had just opened up to **one** person about how much I was struggling, I could have ventured on the road to recovery sooner. It really is true that the first step to overcoming a problem is admitting that you have a problem.

Wherever I could show up pretending that I didn't have a problem, I was still in denial and this thing could grip me tighter than ever. It still had control. I thought I was in control because I was the one getting rid of the junk and starting with a clean slate again and again, but the truth is I could not control the temptations and would give in in utter weakness, so I didn't have to endure the pain of resistance. Having the food and going on a binge, knowing that it would eventually end and my cravings would be satisfied was way easier than fighting the urge, staying strong and holding my place as someone who wanted to be well.

I wanted to be well. I was so intensely desperate to be well. But I wasn't willing to admit to anyone (or myself) that I had a big problem. I feel for the people close to me who may have wanted me to open up and admit my struggles but didn't know how to approach the subject. I also wonder how people would respond if I did open up and they didn't feel equipped to be able to help or support.

I stayed unwell.

Carrathool days led to Chris working on a farming property just outside of Darlington Point, so after a while of daily travel, we were offered a farm cottage to live in and I could get a job at Coleambally. This was 2003; I was 18 turning 19, and Chris was almost 22.

Our social life on the farm was not as full as when we were in town, so weekends were a bit more chill. We could do little

homemaking jobs, visit Bunnings, tinker around the yard together or take the dog down to the river, which wrapped the property we were living on. On weekdays we were working hard and looking forward to the weekend for our chill time.

My mornings would start with a coffee and a cigarette, vowing to eat 'good' today and not derail. This was so easy to claim and declare in my mind while there was no force of temptation and weakness, but as soon as I was caught off guard, the plan was out the window, and I would resolve to start again tomorrow. Most of the time I could obviously mask the symptoms, but what was happening on the inside was indescribable.

I worked diligently and focused for the most part. We were in an office with plenty of other staff members, so visiting the lunch room at morning tea time was a lovely social interaction and often met with someone celebrating a birthday or something delicious, where I could politely decline – 'Not for me, thank you. I'm OK.'

Really, I didn't want it because I was scared. I was scared that that one taste of indulgence would send me into a spiral and spin me out of control, and I wouldn't focus for the rest of the day. It was easier to decline the offer. I was met with comments like 'Oh, I guess that's why you're skinny and I'm not. I have to have the piece of cake' and 'Gosh, you're so good. You have so much self-control. I wish I had that, but it's just too good.'

In my mind, I respond with, 'Oh I love the foods and I appreciate good-tasting bad-for-you cakes and slices, but I can't trust myself to just have a little bit and go on with my day, so it's best not to have any at all.'

Enough With the Lies

If only I had said 'I'm addicted to sugar. I struggle every day with food, and I don't want to fight anymore!', maybe I would have found healing sooner. Instead, I kept quiet and held the badge of being 'so good and self-controlled'.

Of course, I felt in control. In a room of colleagues who claimed they couldn't resist the piece of cake, I was the one who could. Yay me, so strong and so powerful. On the outside, yes, it appears that way. Inside my mind and body – complete turmoil and destruction, not knowing what was going to happen next or when I would get my next alone time.

I was like a fat kid trapped in my thin and fit-looking body. Usually, if there was a teaser or taste during the day, it would then stage out to nibbling away all afternoon until I got home when I could properly binge and go overboard and get rid of it all.

I hate to think of the amount of money I wasted and blew on rubbish from the supermarket. I had a 25-minute drive home each day and would often get home before Chris, so I would be able to munch away on the way home (after barely eating anything all day) and know that I had a chance to explode my desires when I got home – and was alone. I would pig out on cake when no one was around (mostly uncooked cake batter, freshly made icing, or a bucket-load of ice cream), I would binge on sugary alcohol and indulge in midnight feasts at the end of a big night out on the town, then I would guzzle almost a litre of fizzy drink at a time just to empty out my stomach and 'wash away' all the food so it wouldn't have a chance to enter my digestive system and be processed by my body, causing me to have the effects of a little weight gain or anything like that.

enough

My self-control was a **mess**. The slightest thing would derail me, so the longer I could hold it off, the longer I could stay on track and feel like I was beating it (and not that it was beating me). But each time, I gathered myself back into perfection, hid all the signs, stashed all the evidence and carried on like life was rosy.

I never really found that I had to lie so much about it as I was just so cunning at sneaking it. There was nothing to deny if I hid it well enough not to cause any suspicion.

I hate to think of the physical state of my body from a medical perspective because I put my body through hell. Whatever was in my stomach, if I filled it full enough, could be emptied, and then I would start again. Clean slate. I would promise myself – lie to myself, more like it – that from **now** on, I would eat perfect, I would do this right, I would not mess it up, I wouldn't eat any bad foods. I'd be good with my eating.

Of course, that worked most of the time when I was around other people, but on my own, the temptation was too strong, the cravings debilitating. I couldn't function until I had the thing that led to another thing and another, until I couldn't physically fit any more. I would bounce from sweet to savoury and back again, indulging in the chaos of my cravings. I was chasing the desire like a drug addict chasing the next hit.

I'm sure there were resources and support that could have helped me, but I wasn't willing to admit my full struggle.

Pride stopped me from being real.

Fear stopped me from opening up, so I kept quiet.

Enough With the Lies

I wanted so desperately to break this cycle. I wanted to stop with the hiding. I wanted it all to just stop – but I was the one making the choices. While I didn't consciously decide I wanted to go on a binge, it was a repeated pattern that I fell into and knew that ultimately I was the only one who could have stopped it.

I placed so much pressure on myself that I hated myself at an even deeper level every time I repeated behaviours. I honestly don't think there was a single day that I didn't throw up. It was constant bursts of gutsing followed by a weighty burden of guilt and shame and helplessness.

Chris and I were planning our wedding for April 2005, and I promised myself that I would get better before our wedding so that my eyes weren't so sunken and my face wasn't so puffy. I was imagining that I would be a glow of health and not the dark-circled puffy-eyed mess I'd become. I wanted energy and vibrance, but I was far from it. I remember preparing for our wedding day; it was November 2004, and I only had five months to sort myself out. I'd been scrapbooking my ideas, making bonbonniere, writing my speech and dreaming about all the trimmings of the day.

One Friday night, Chris went out shooting with a friend, and we received a phone call that his older brother John had taken his own life. My insides churned at the reality and painfulness of it. I cannot even describe what it feels like to lose someone in those circumstances, and I cannot imagine how intensely it has affected Chris and his family. John was 34. He left behind three children who were 10, 9 and 6 at the time. My reality check at that moment was that 'This is what I am doing – I am

enough

slowly killing myself. It's slow suicide. I have to stop. There has to be a way out.'

Again, no loving support or encouragement from myself to make lasting change, just a condemning 'pull yourself together, snap out of it, get over it, wake up' slap in the face. Not kind at all.

We journeyed through the days and weeks following John's passing, and it all seems like a bit of a blur. Questions around suicide are huge. Why? Who could have helped? Why didn't we know? Could anyone have stopped him?

It's not something that was easy to process and, in leading up to our wedding, it rocked both our perspectives. We had no idea John was struggling the way he did, and with any form of mental illness, if the person is suffering enough, they will find a way to hide it well.

No one will ever know the depths of pain within his mind and heart. I empathise with John now, but at the time, it was a scary reality that his internal dialogue could be that dark and messed up and he was not able to see a way out. I still wanted a way out of my darkness, although I believed I was the only one who could navigate it.

Christmas happened.

April came around. We were finally getting married.

I still was not better.

CHAPTER 4

It's All Good on the Outside

Chris and I took a couple of days to get away after our wedding. We booked ourselves a honeymoon for July (a better time on the farmers' calendar to get away).

In September, we purchased a home in Darlington Point and returned to town life. We both kept the same jobs we were in; it was only 10 kilometres for Chris to get to work and around 30 kilometres for me. Like before, living in town increased our social life. Chris joined the football club and landed some good mates to hang out with. Conveniently, our home fronted onto the back of the golf course and sports club. This invited easy access to Thursday night club raffles, Friday night draws, Saturday afternoon happy hour and Sunday football drinks. Sometimes I would go with Chris and the crew to the club for their drinking sessions, but many times I opted to stay home (like many of the other girlfriends) and isolate myself.

We didn't have kids. I wasn't part of any sport. My alone time was an isolation period where I would default to the binge and throw-up cycle. Sometimes I would do creative projects like scrapbooking or just potter around the house. But mostly I binged myself out of existence. I could occasionally be done with a binge by 8 pm and then join the party at the club and drink my way through the night with everyone else, partying and living like all the other young people in town. My shoulders would bear knots so tight and tense from the convulsions, I don't think I ever relaxed. The social scene was fun, and I loved each and every person we hung out with, but deep down I still hated myself.

Chris and I had talked about starting a family, but it wasn't on the immediate radar. Our plan was to start a family, but we wanted to settle into the 'us' life as adults a bit longer and set up a bit of financial stability. Having just purchased our home meant we needed both incomes, and we needed to get ahead financially before committing to welcoming a baby.

We joked that Chris wanted more time to **not** have to share his toys, and I wanted more time to get in a better financial position to be able to fully commit and devote my time to being a mum without having to sacrifice time with the baby to go back to work. I wanted to be a full-time stay-at-home mum more than anything.

It sounded like a wonderful plan. Meanwhile, we were both binge drinking every Thursday to Sunday, not really being very adulty, but we were having fun (and, in our defence, still so young).

The payments on the house were a whole new thing. We'd been living rent–free (in Carrathool and then on the farm) for a few years, and the shock of weekly loan payment plus rates, insurance, maintenance, Bunnings visits and many more all began to hit my cautious buttons. This didn't help my hidden anxious state.

One day in 2006, I found an ad in the paper (yes, this is how old I am!) that said, '**Earn extra income;** work from home'. It hooked my curiosity and propelled my desperation, so I made a phone call during my lunchbreak and went through the process to find out how I could make extra income on top of my full–time job. I was basically assured that this would be an amazing fit for what I was looking for and was convinced we could smash out our home loan and start our family sooner than expected.

From this ad, I was introduced to Herbalife, a network marketing company with a line of nutritional health supplements. This was the business opportunity – take the products, love them, share them with friends and family, earn commission.

I purchased my starter pack in secrecy. Why I wanted to be secretly earning, I'm not quite sure. I think I wanted to be the hero that provided the lifestyle I hoped was possible. I thought I had something to prove – maybe to myself. A big part of me also didn't want to tell anyone in case I failed at this. Secrecy was part of my identity by then, and

enough

I didn't know any different; I was so buried in shame and low self-worth.

So, I had a plan – a secret plan. I would out-earn myself from my current job, position us enough to safely take time off to start a family and not miss out on any lifestyle luxuries. My desire was to enjoy quality time as a family without having to go to a real job and not have any financial worries.

My problem was that I wanted to earn all this extra income, yet I didn't want to tell anyone close to me. I had no idea that authenticity would be a major part of my success. The problem with starting a business and not wanting to share it openly is that no one knows what you do. You can't build traffic to drive sales if no one knows what you have to offer.

Over the years, I've tried so many things to become financially free. And when I say *tried*, I mean 'gone to grab the thing, then dreamed and imagined and hoped but never really fully passionately took any action'. So, it took me a while to find what works.

Turns out, anything works when I work.

I wasn't willing to do the work. The hard work was uncomfortable, and I didn't like being uncomfortable. I was more comfortable in my mess than I was digging myself out of it.

Since I discovered the Herbalife products for the business opportunity and convinced myself that I could help people improve their health and reach the healthy weight and optimum body state they desired, I felt like a fraud. I wasn't even living fully and wholly healthy. How could I help someone else when I was so far from perfect? How could I help people manage their weight? No one is going to listen to me; I've never had a weight problem. I've always been thin. I can't relate to the people who are overweight, so they won't buy from me.

My health was a mess, but thankfully, due to the absorption of nutrition I was getting, I gained some energy and vibrance back. The products were amazing, honestly. If I didn't have that foundational top–up of nutrition every day, who knows what extent of deeper damage I would have faced from my condition? I took the products anyway and fell in love with the simplicity. I also fell in love with the extra cover–up – I can eat whatever I want and throw it all up and then begin again with this highly nutritious meal in a drink, and I have the nourishment my body needs for the day! I can 'not eat' and still survive the day.

A perfect cover–up to the damage and strain I am putting my body through? Yesss, please!

Little did I know what was going on with my hormones or gut health or brain chemicals. I could have my cake, eat it too, and throw it up and cover it up with this nutrition powerhouse and no one would know. Sweet! Yes, they were sweet too, which meant I could go to work in the morning, have a decadent chocolate cookies and cream milkshake for breakfast and not have guilt. Winning!

I crafted my story so that people would know the products saved me, then everyone would want them. I tried the path of 'this product helped me overcome my eating disorder' (which it didn't) and shared a little bit of my story, but I didn't share fully because I hadn't recovered. This was another delusion

enough

of mine. I was still suffering. It was too shameful to admit I was still stuck in this. I tried to bluff my way out of being unwell. I imagined this sickness into being, surely I could imagine it out.

What I didn't realise was that taking these Herbalife products, a meal replacement and nutritional supplement line, was probably what saved me from fully destroying my body as I continued to throw up. Whenever I was empty and not holding any food down, the supplements supported me to feel 'OK' rather than feeling almost dead from getting hit by a truck, which I had been feeling for six years.

It was around this time that I began to appreciate my health a little bit and paid more attention to eating some nourishing foods to help support my body. The Herbalife shakes provided a way of escape for me to continue doing what I was doing in secret and no one would find out. I was the healthy shake lady. I looked healthy. I was thin. Fit–looking. I was inspiring others to look after their health.

I transformed from someone who never ate breakfast and only had a cigarette and coffee on the way to work to someone who bought fresh fruits. We never had fresh fruit growing up – maybe because we lived rationally and out of tins – but trying to fit in whole fresh fruits was a challenge. They were going off in the fruit bowl before we got to them.

It was hard to throw up fresh fruit, especially apples, so that was the last thing I was willing to consume if there was a chance I'd be trying to unpack later in the day.

It's All Good on the Outside

I started running in the morning with our dog, mostly to get her the exercise she was missing being in town now. Every morning I'd get up early and go out in the cold to do a few laps around the block.

Leaning into the philosophies of Herbalife and living a healthy lifestyle, I really enjoyed this. It ignited a passion that feeling good and looking after myself is rewarding and life-giving. While I increased this part of my healthy lifestyle plan, I still offset it with destructive behaviours and didn't fully experience the benefits I could have. On the outside looking in, though, I seemed to have it all together.

But I was not being honest about my whole situation. They didn't know I struggle with binge eating like anyone struggling with weight, but that's not open for discussion. Whenever I was lying to myself and others around me, I was not walking in integrity, therefore blocking any flow of blessing that would come through sharing the products.

Herbalife was how I discovered the true importance of nutrition. What I didn't realise at the time was that my journey and experience with Herbalife played a pivotal role in my physical healing and created a safety buffer for a very long time. That meant my illness didn't show to the world as much as it would have if I had kept going the way I was. Perhaps the fact that I began to open up and share small pieces of my story also helped reduce the intensity of my condition.

As a result of joining Herbalife, I began my journey of deeper learning into the body and nutrition and understanding the science of how our body systems function. Suddenly, I was being educated and interested in our bodies.

enough

Still, I secretly looked for help, trying to understand the whole bulimia eating disorder category. I didn't fit any of the criteria. Most of the girls and women I read about were struggling with identity and body image issues and were concerned about getting fat. I wasn't worried about that. Although, I controlled it by purging all the food I ate.

My battle was with food addiction – the temptation and torment of the food, the confinement of being a slave to my cravings. The only reason I would get rid of it all was because I didn't want to get overweight, yes, but I couldn't work out why I kept on eating food anyway. It wasn't like I was eating a regular meal and then scared of the calories, so I would throw it up. I was actually searching out extra-calorie foods and pigging my little guts out to satisfy some kind of crazy addiction. I didn't know why, but the temptation was strong.

My issue was not a body image eating disorder. I wasn't 'one of them'. So, again, I didn't get the help I needed.

I didn't talk about it. I kept it secret and stayed in my shame tank with all the guilt and embarrassment for my actions and behaviours. On the occasions when I could bluff my way through social situations, I was free to do whatever I wanted when I was alone. What I wanted was full blocks of chocolate, whole tubs of ice cream, cake batter, nachos and, if I was desperate and out of junk food, porridge with loads of brown sugar.

Erghh! My stomach feels queasy at the thought of that now, but at the time I wanted **all** of it and I wanted the **richest** form of indulgence I could get. But that was embarrassing to admit, so I didn't tell anyone.

Food became good and bad. There was a list of naughty and nice.

Midway through 2006, Chris changed jobs from the farm at Darlington Point to a property at Coleambally, which is closer to where I was working. This landed us back in a farmhouse, and so we had an opportunity to rent our house out. Rent income covered the cost of the home loan, so I was pretty happy about that. My drive and desperation to have the business opportunity work relaxed, and I dwindled in enthusiasm.

I wasn't believing in myself. That has been my biggest letdown.

Whenever anything became uncomfortable, I would squirm and retreat back to safety … and life on the farm was safe. We didn't have the financial stress of making full house repayments, so we were comfortable again.

In 2007, we started trying for a baby. I was 23 when I stopped taking the contraceptive pill.

We struggled to conceive, and I blamed myself.

It was my fault. This damage I had caused to my body was catching up to me.

More guilt.

More shame.

More feeling of no control.

enough

My periods were completely abnormal and unpredictable. There was nothing the medical system could draw from in terms of what my hormones were doing. Their first assurance was that since I had been taking the contraceptive pill for seven years, it would take a fair while for my hormones to return to their usual rhythm and present fertile. We just had to wait it out.

I had zero idea that my **emotions** and my **mind** were driving most of this. If I had dug into the mess within my soul and mind and addressed the root causes of my feelings and thoughts causing my actions, I would have experienced healing and freedom so much sooner.

Ever since those teenage years, whenever I had an emotion, I ignored it, tried to suppress it and then messed myself up physically. Now the emotional feeling wasn't the problem; it became a physical problem to deal with. The emotions were buried in the rubble.

At times, I felt physically OK. I was completely oblivious to the presence of my emotions, then more cravings would come (unknowingly driven by the emotions I hadn't dealt with), so the spiral of binge, purge, cry, pity, shame, guilt and condemnation would slam me to my lowest point again. Lower than I'd ever been.

Every time I rose up to overcome, the fall back into the pit was deeper and darker than ever before.

I truly thought there was no coming back, I'd gone too far in the wrong direction. Yet, I refused to turn around because I didn't believe I was worthy of walking the high road to peak health and an abundant life. Plus, it seemed too hard. I felt like there was no hope, darkened and doomed by my own actions and messed up belief system.

After another move and Chris changing jobs from Coleambally to Hillston, I became a stay-at-home wife (hoping and wishing it would be a stay-at-home mum role very soon).

Our hope was deferred.

I continued to struggle.

I'm not sure if I had opened up again to Chris at this stage. I didn't want to hurt him any more than I already had. This secrecy and shame and hiding was too much to own up to. I really believed I had messed up way too bad.

I had mornings at Hillston where I would get up early with Chris, start my day by walking the dog, have a cup of tea and tidy the house, then wonder what on earth I was meant to be doing. I questioned what my life was. What was the point of my existence? It was very lonely and very confusing. I thought by now we would have easily fallen pregnant. I thought by now I would have some kind of purpose worked out. Yet, here I was, circling this mountain of destruction without a way of undoing the mess I had created.

I went down the path of trying to find out if there was anything more physical to explain why I wasn't having my monthly cycle and why we hadn't conceived. There were a few medical things we could check, like hormone levels, cysts or conditions that might be preventing ovulation, but nothing severe was announced. **Not knowing** what the

enough

problem is, when you clearly know there is a problem, is worse than having a name for your problem and being able to find resources to solve it.

After almost 12 months of being at Hillston, where I had eventually gathered a few casual jobs to get my mind off this whole starting a family project, we decided to move to Gundagai for Chris's job as a Farm Manager. During the job interview we discovered there was a contract for an admin position over at Tumut, working alongside the farm owners Chris would be working for, so it was like a package deal. We both had secure jobs to go to and a farmhouse just out of Gundagai, an hour from Wagga Wagga.

I was on the waitlist to receive treatment for checking my reproductive system and had been prescribed some Clomid, which was meant to help induce ovulation. We openly shared with our new employers that we were trying for a family and that I would not continue working if that happened. They were OK with that, and it felt so good to be open and transparent about something.

The Clomid was a horrific experience for me. As well as still suffering with my eating disorder, I dove into a deep, dark depression, to the point that Chris said, 'We don't have to have kids. This is not worth it. I would rather have us than lose ourselves trying for this baby.'

I hesitantly agreed. I could not imagine my lifetime without children, so I imagined the idea of fostering or working in childcare forever. But he was right. Going completely mental was not worth it. I had to surrender my control and release my desperation.

It's All Good on the Outside

In January 2009, I fell pregnant with our first baby, George. There was a glimmer of hope. My self-pity shifted into the realisation that someone else's life now depended on me. And I recovered. I believed, all of a sudden, that more love was possible.

I'd been listening to a lot of self-help stuff, reading books, journalling (mostly condemning myself and declaring I'd never do it again, then apologising when I did). My soul was searching, and I began to understand the mess that was in my mind.

My pregnancy was a surprise, as I still hadn't had any periods. I thought it must have been a result of the 'I'm worth it' mantras I was beginning to believe. Later, I knew it was a gift from God.

At the time, my encounter with self-love was producing results and I could then give and receive love at a deeper level. I could love myself, love this unborn child of ours and experience the depth of love my husband had been offering all along.

My mind still continually defaulted to negative and destructive thoughts, but I was developing the skill of reframing and changing how I spoke to myself. I became slightly comfortable with my own company rather than trying to escape myself. I felt like I wasn't alone anymore.

For such a long time, I wrestled, struggled and fought with this mental war that beat me over and over again. Then, just like that, in the line of a positive pregnancy test, I was cured. No longer bulimic. No longer a sufferer. I was a victor, not a victim.

This pregnancy and change in direction was a complete turnaround in my mental health. My physical health benefited, too, as I lovingly nourished my body and listened to what it was telling me throughout the pregnancy.

My pregnancy was a breeze. Apart from the initial 17 weeks of nausea and not feeling great all day, I felt so alive and so strong and capable and blessed. I was humbled by the blessing, as this was **not** something I willed into existence. It was a true gift after two years of no answers and no control. I did not deserve this, but I desired it so strongly.

George, a healthy 8-pound baby, was born naturally in October 2009. Life felt complete. I was so in awe at this new life and the intricacies of how life begins. The fact that I could exist day after day and not even face any temptation that I fought with for so long blew my mind.

This experience was evidence to me that I could exist and not be controlled by the food cravings and temptations. I had proof. I didn't need the binges and fixes any more.

It's quite easy and natural to get caught up in the hustle of whatever chaos we have going on in our lives. It's easy to get buried by the fast pace and busyness of the season, but when you take a moment to look around and breathe in pure gratitude for the blessings laid out before you, you can't help but wonder – Why? How? Can I be so loved?

Gratitude is not just a thought of thankfulness. True gratitude is a heart-tingling feeling that changes you from the inside out. It's a *being*, not a *doing*.

It's All Good on the Outside

When you are being thankful or grateful, allow yourself enough depth to really let it land.

Life is fleeting.

Don't let your moments fly by.

Breathe them in.

CHAPTER 5

Finding Hope in the Hopelessness

As we revelled in this new life together as a family, I was in a bliss state – full-time mum at home enjoying our baby. I was still dabbling with the idea that I could create financial freedom for us through a side hustle but not one bit intrinsically motivated to do the hard work to achieve success.

Journalling was my therapy. I would write all of my ponderings, and then I would write all the wisdom that came to me. This was so incredibly helpful and powerful, as I began to see that sharing my journey and being transparent will help others. I knew then that I wanted to write my book. I started sharing openly about my struggles with a few close family and friends. This was easier since I had come out the other side.

enough

Being in the depths of it, I carried so much guilt and shame around it being an issue. Looking back now, I wish I had opened up sooner. Way sooner – like every time it gripped me from the very first time, it started to take me over again. I **know** for sure that if I had spoken about it and brought it into the light, I would not have felt so alone and afraid. I wouldn't have been tormented in the dark.

When George was 13 months old, Chris made another advance in his career and accepted a manager's position on a property called Dolgelly, an hour out of Moree in northern NSW. This was 1,000 kilometres from our parents and all of our family and friends scattered throughout Goolgowi, Carrathool, Darlington Point, Coleambally, Hillston and now Gundagai and Wagga.

I had recently returned to a couple days of work at Tumut, and George was in daycare for those days. We also decided to purchase an investment property in Tumut using the equity of our Darlington Point house. We had received a lot of advice from colleagues that real estate was a good investment, and while we had on–farm accommodation, it was a good use of our money to have something later in life to fall back on if farming was not Chris's career choice.

We locked into five years of an interest–only loan to finance two adjoining flats in Tumut. As I was at home with George, and Chris and I planned on having more babies, this seemed like the best way to go for cashflow.

We learned so much from this experience; we didn't really do our research or look intently at the numbers or do our calculations well. We simply trusted the advice from others and believed that, long term, it was the way to go.

Finding Hope in the Hopelessness

I still had a hunger and a desire to create wealth working from home, flexibly and around family, but whenever I hit a pain point in the learning process, I would shrink back. I had a lot of learning (and unlearning) to do. This pattern got worse and worse the longer I let it rule and unconsciously just ran with the commentary that 'This is how I am. I'm not good at these things'. The yearning was still there, though, and so it popped up with a little confidence every now and then. And then I would become defeated again. Generally, I found myself drawn to the things I was naturally good at and had confidence I could do well without fail. My perfect streak tendencies ruled.

Our new home at Dolgelly was pretty amazing. It was like station life. We were an hour from any town (Goondiwindi to the north of us, Moree to the south), with half of the travel time spent on rough gravel roads. We had a massive home with wide wraparound, enclosed verandas and an in-ground pool coming off the side. There was an office and formal dining, with an extra wing of the house that was probably the butler's or cleaner's living space back in the day. Just the three of us in this massive home, more than 10 hours away from our family and friends. It was a chapter neither of us were ready for.

Chris's role was certainly much more managerial in the office than any previous job he had worked on. There was another staff member who also lived on the property, in the cottage right next to ours. The farm was owned by an old lady in Sydney, and her two 60-year-old sons controlled the company, overseeing Chris and the consultancy team to operate the farm profitability. There were sheep as well as mixed dryland cropping, so there was quite a variety of work for Chris all year round and plenty of exciting things for George and me

to explore when we were bored at home. We could drive around for miles and still not see all of the property.

I settled into the station life with a routine to visit Moree just once a fortnight to get groceries and do town jobs. There was a beautiful little playgroup at a nearby school (40 kilometres from home) I was invited to by one of the neighbours. It was a very welcoming community but far between most properties. A visit for a cuppa was usually at least a half-day outing, and going to town was a whole-day adventure. We did have a couple of neighbours, just a few kilometres from home, whom I got to spend a fair bit of time with. They had a little boy younger than George, so it didn't feel that isolating.

In early February of 2011, we found out that I was pregnant again. This was on our radar since George was about 11 months old when I weaned him, trying to get my body and my cycle back to normal again (even though there never was any normal). We knew, being such a struggle the first time around, that we had to give ourselves plenty of time for things to happen and create a nice space in between siblings. The anticipation of another baby coming along was exciting. I knew that I wasn't going back to work; we were confident that Chris's income could support us, and we had tenants in all three properties, so they were taken care of.

Somewhere during the pregnancy, I relapsed into binge eating and found myself having bursts of gorging on sweet foods until the point of throwing up. I had no idea why. I paid little attention to what my body was telling me or what was going on in my emotional and mental health. I immediately resorted to condemnation and harsh inner critic talk.

Finding Hope in the Hopelessness

Words like *You're hopeless, useless, weak, no good* all consumed my thinking. I fully blamed myself. The fact that this was happening while I was growing a baby, I felt intensely bad that I might have been doing something to hurt the baby. The thing is, I couldn't stop. I didn't want to ask for help or tell Chris again because I felt like such a failure. I knew that he would ask why, and I knew that my answer was 'I don't know, but I hate myself for it.' It was more comfortable to keep quiet and not burden anyone else. I could overcome this again on my own. Well, that's what I told myself anyway.

I juggled our budget on a month–by–month basis, making sure there were enough funds to buy groceries every fortnight. Chris's salary was monthly, and the rent came in monthly. The repayments for the home loans also came out monthly, so it all happened at the end of the month.

For some reason, we were slowly but surely dwindling backwards in funds left over each month. I sensed a tightening of losing control of our finances, and the fear of that drove me again to become desperate in needing to make some source of income.

I dabbled with some random things online, looking and hoping that I would land on 'the one' that delivered on its promise and worked for us. This actually put us into more debt; however, I hadn't told Chris about the required investment because I thought I could get us out of it. I did zero deep work on myself and had very little self–awareness of my beliefs and behaviours. I would quickly default to thinking and believing that I was no good, that my imperfections and shortcomings were faults and that there was something terribly wrong with me.

enough

My pregnancy was again relatively good. I didn't binge and throw up every single day like before, but I found that opportunities of loneliness and not wanting to be in my own company had me falling into a heap quite regularly with my eating.

I remember the guilt and heavy shame weighing me down so badly. One day, after a couple of days of repeated bingeing, I was an emotional mess –crying uncontrollably at the fact I kept on doing this to myself (and our unborn baby!). I wanted to close my eyes to escape completely and then wake up and never have to face food again. I wrestled with the thought that having a terminal illness or extreme diagnosis of something physical would be better. At least, then, it wouldn't be my fault. It wouldn't be in my control.

Looking back now, I can see so clearly that all of this behaviour was driven by my inability to regulate my emotions. I was continually letting my suppressed feelings dictate my thoughts. I tried changing my thoughts, but the force was way too strong for anything that I tried to work for any period of time.

I ended up discovering a mother's group in Goondiwindi through a community booklet when we first moved. A group of women held Bible studies every fortnight and, in between, had coffee–and–chat mornings. George and I (and my growing pregnant tummy) were welcomed in with loving, open arms. Amazing friendships grew from this fortnightly catch–up, and I had found a support network that comprised of mother figures, aunties and sisters. This community allowed me space to share and observe things about myself that I had no awareness of previously. I'd describe it like the village we need to raise a family. Our kids all played together, and we shared birthdays and play dates whenever we could.

Finding Hope in the Hopelessness

That August, we celebrated Chris's 30th birthday on the property, inviting friends and family from down south to come and see our new life. Our niece, Melinda (the one who lost her dad to suicide), came to stay with us for a few weeks. She was 15 at the time. A beautiful girl, so broken and so lost but just like a regular 15-year-old, dealing with all the usual teenage things. Minnie, as we call her, had been through so much we would never be able to comprehend.

It was a good time for us as a family to spend that time observing her around George and witness their cousin love that was instantaneous and natural. Minnie's mum had shared with us that they were having a hard time with her. She thought that spending time with Chris would be healing for her.

Minnie was a typical teenage girl, snacking on Coco Pops at 10.30 at night and wanting to sleep in until 11 am. She was moody and unpredictable – fun-loving, then miserable. All pretty normal behaviour to me, although I was so disconnected from what being a normal teenager was like. I spent my teen years completely numbing myself from any of my emotions. And here I was as an adult going to a place of escape, needing rehab or abstinence or something, but I couldn't abstain. I needed food.

We can't just give up food like an alcoholic gives up alcohol. I couldn't just avoid it and be clean. No matter how much I tried to start the clean slate and do it right, each day my cravings crept in more frequently, and I felt myself losing the battle. My desperation to be well but inability to know **how** was crushing me. I felt like such a failure.

Claire was born perfectly healthy in September 2011. Soon after she was born, I went for the Implanon rod for contraception.

enough

We hadn't used any form of contraception since going off the pill in 2007, and the rod was recommended as a hassle-free fit by doctors and midwives.

About six weeks into having the Implanon inserted, I recognised I was not in a good place. I had struggled with Claire settling and having a good routine. It was hard to get her to sleep, and it was very different to what we experienced with George. I didn't particularly notice my mental health declining, but I vividly remember one morning laying in bed after a couple of feeds through the night, 2-year-old George came and crawled into our bed. I pulled the blankets over my head and had this horrific feeling that I didn't want to face the day today. His delight and joy were repulsing me, and I was so super cranky. I didn't want to see Claire, I didn't want to see him, I just wanted to escape back into my sleep where there was no day to face and disappear. This was so scary.

Along with struggling with my eating again, I didn't feel like I could be honest about this because I felt responsible. I was creating these thoughts. I studied that I could change my thoughts, but the fact that I was having them made me feel like a failure and like I'd messed up way too much.

I did a little googling to find out about my symptoms and resolved that the Implanon was wreaking havoc with my (already messed up) hormones. I booked a doctor's appointment to get it out, and they said it would be a good idea to let it stay in and wait it out a bit longer for things to settle.

I was so afraid that things were not going to settle. It was the most awful feeling I've ever felt (and maybe the most attuned I had ever been to my feelings). I knew I needed it out.

Finding Hope in the Hopelessness

'Someone is going to die – either myself, my baby, my toddler or my husband. I feel **that** bad! I am so nasty and mean, and I can't go on with this!' I said to the doctor.

Thankfully, they heard me, and I had it removed. It reminded me of the Clomid experience all over again, only this time I was riding the rollercoaster of a toddler and a newborn and a husband under increasing pressure at work with no family support or no old-time friends to escape to. We were so far out of our depth. The financial tightening also meant that a big trip home to visit family or friends was not an option just yet.

Luckily, I had my support network from my Bible study group. When an intense financial breakdown happened to us in March 2012, one of the ladies prayed for me and invited me into a personal relationship with Jesus. I discovered my deep faith from then on. I began attending their Bible study to learn more about this concept of faith that I knew very little about.

My heart had always been searching. I had been on a spiritual journey, exploring things like clairvoyants and fortune tellers and learning about chakras and the third eye. I really had no idea how light or dark these things were, but I could see that these women had something about them, something bigger than themselves – a connection to a power far greater than me. It made me realise I needed to be able to trust in something bigger because I had proven time and time again that I couldn't rely on myself. I was hopelessly messing up my life. If this was an opportunity to surrender, release control and believe that God loves me more than I could ever love myself, then I wanted to know for sure it was real. Nothing I had sought so far had filled the void.

Chris was not very accommodating of my newfound faith. This was the biggest test we had ever faced in our relationship. He was really, really against it. He didn't like religion (and I don't blame him; religion has a lot to answer for), and this God/Jesus invading our home was a very confronting time for him.

I began to understand that God is way bigger than any problem we face and any difference we encounter as humans, so my journey to surrender and trust became more profound than ever. My desire to get well and get out of the mess we were in was stronger than ever. The fact that I was still hiding things from Chris but discovering that I couldn't hide **anything** from God, yet He still loved me like crazy allowed me to resolve that Chris's love for me was strong enough for me to own up and confess again what I had been doing. This was hard – really uncomfortable, sickening, gut-wrenchingly hard.

Chris himself was suffering with his own battles. I don't think he fully grieved the loss of his brother, and I think the more he grew older and wiser, the more he probably needed an older brother to reach out to and say, 'Hey, how do we do this?', but that was not an option. Plus, we were living thousands of kilometres away from the usual hangout crowd of friends and still establishing our place in the community we were now in. It was a hard gig for Chris. Meanwhile, his wife and best friend was losing her sanity and reaching for the Bible.

My faith experience was certainly not a 'find yourself a Jesus, and all your problems go away' situation; I don't know anybody who has experienced that. But as I pieced the puzzle together and gradually, moment by moment, let God love me and uncover my true identity, I cannot describe the change in my soul that had me clinging to a hope I never thought was possible. I thought all this time I had to save myself, I had to get myself out of this mess and make up for all of the mistakes I made.

You know what? I will **never** be able to pay back all of the wrongs that I have done in my life, to myself and to those who love me. And I thank God that I don't have to, because Jesus paid the price for the wrong we've done, and whenever we walk in unity with him, turn to God and be open and honest about our hearts, we can remain faithful to Him and live freely as we were created to live from the beginning.

I didn't know how to express myself properly except through written words. I continued to journal and extract wisdom from my heart while I journeyed into this unknown experience. The only way I knew how to express to Chris what was going on was to write him a letter, pouring my heart out and confessing the habits I had fallen into again. I wrote this letter and then went on a big trip with the two kids to attend a friend's wedding and visit family back home. Chris was coming down for the wedding too, but he didn't have the two-week window of time like I did because of work. We both agreed it would be a good idea to have some space and spend a bit of time apart to let things settle down.

We weren't talking at home. I felt so bad. I didn't want to drive him away. I didn't know that my own pain and internal struggle would have such an impact on him. I loved him so, so much and yet I couldn't work out why he would love me back. I felt so unlovable and had done so wrong by him over the years with all of this secrecy and hiding. The guilt was killing me. My pride was keeping me stuck.

enough

I later found out that Chris thought that was the end of us. He thought I was going to visit family and not come home. He thought I was done with him and giving up on us. Meanwhile, I was done with myself, but again, still, I couldn't get away from myself. The only way to get away from myself was to get closer to myself and face my baggage – something I had never ever done before. I didn't want to do that; it was too uncomfortable and unfamiliar. It felt unsafe.

We played the happy family during our visit and had an amazing time catching up with long–lost friends at the wedding, but going back home to Dolgelly was the most awkward thing. I started questioning if I had used up all of Chris's love for me. I'd wasted it throughout all these years of being so self–absorbed, self–focused, absent and numb. I thought I had created such a chasm between us, that nothing could bring us back together or heal or repair what I had done.

I talked to no one about this. My new faith community knew that I was at the beginning of my journey to discover who God had created me to be, and they were so loving and so supportive and just so deeply real. I had never ever felt I could be so real and raw before. I could share all of it, and I was met with a level of compassion and a glimmer of hope with each pain I shared.

I still struggled with my eating because it was one thing I thought was too big to deal with. I believed I wasn't able to fight through, so it was easier to suffer. Although I initially held doubt towards my decision to explore my faith, because I had proven myself to not make very good choices in the past, I knew there was something (or someone) greater than me that could provide me the strength I needed.

Finding Hope in the Hopelessness

As my confidence grew in being able to trust my own judgement and take those small steps out of my comfort zone, I pressed further into understanding the Bible and the principles of God and, most powerfully, the presence of God. I began to really trust God, but I didn't do it openly in our home so that I wouldn't offend Chris and cause more tension. He was hurting enough. I was hurting. Our kids needed us. We couldn't get away.

I came to the revelation that God is so much bigger than anything we face on earth, so I held on. God could carry the weight of my guilt and shame and torment. Chris couldn't … and shouldn't have to. God could restore our marriage, even though it felt like the very thing creating a wedge between us.

My bulimia didn't immediately go away. I was saved from sin but not free from myself. The next decade of my journey would reveal that the war in my mind was a battleground for the enemy. I still had a long way to go. Even today, as I write this part of my story and reflect, I acknowledge I still have a long way to go. But I have hope, and that is the best.

What I began to learn during these Bible study sessions hit me with so much realisation as to what was going on inside my mind, body and soul. I slowly began to understand that the negative default setting I was continuously running on was **not** God's design or plan for me. God's plan is for truth and life. I was operating under the influence of the enemy, whose plan is to steal, kill and destroy. I was deceived by lies, and I believed these lies were true.

I believed I wasn't good enough. That's not true.

I believed I would mess everything up. That's not true.

enough

I believed I didn't deserve all of the good things in my life. Also not true.

The thing with realising the truth and the lies we believe – it gives us a starting point to decide where we want to go from here. I didn't feel like I was consciously choosing my path. I thought I was a victim; like these things were happening to me. Poor me. Pity me. I'm suffering, and I don't deserve to get out of this place.

As I saw and experienced more truth, I saw and experienced more freedom. There were ways I could resist the desires of my flesh (cravings and temptations) and surrender to the spirit (my soul, my being, my heart). At any moment, I could acknowledge the unconditional love of God for me. When I did this, the temptations fell away. I was not in a struggle and fight for my life. There was a peace. There was freedom. I was no longer a victim of my own thoughts and actions, no longer a slave. But I had to draw my attention there.

It sounds so wonderful to put it so simply, but this was the very beginning of my faith journey, and I had a long way to go. I had a lot to learn and a lot to unlearn. My conditioning from when I was little was so ingrained in me, that never once was there an attempt to correct it (because no one else knew the intensity of it). I never asked for help. I never knew they were lies being wired into my subconscious mind that would ultimately rule my life into self-destruction.

I cannot emphasise enough the importance of **speaking life** into our children; rather than correcting them and arguing against everything they say that does not reflect truth, give them instead a solid foundation of truth to stand on and form their identity on.

Finding Hope in the Hopelessness

You are beautiful. You are loved. You are unique, and you have a purpose. Your thoughts can be transformed. If you notice a thought making you feel a certain way, question it and return to kindness.

We must be kind to ourselves.

The biggest concern in rising anxiety we see today is a result of the inner talk dictated by our feelings. If you are feeling helpless and hopeless, ask **why**. Is that true? What would the creator of the Universe say about you? Because He is the Creator of your life. He has plans for you. There is meaning to your life, and it is filled with goodness, mercy, love, abundance and wholeness. Anything less than that is a disservice to you and your family and those around you. You're being called to step up to the plate and play full out. This life is rich. You deserve its fullness. You are enough.

CHAPTER 6

I'm So Exhausted From the Fight

My journey to get to a place of being able to surrender and let go of the control I had clung to for so long got worse before it got better. The fight became more intense with every move I made closer to God and my relationship with Jesus.

This can be uncomfortable to talk about because not everyone understands the Christian faith. I get that, and I honour and respect that. This is my journey of healing, and I cannot tell it honestly without the bold declaration of my belief in the Word of God being the truth. So much of what I had searched for and looked to for healing and freedom offered only a counterfeit version of what Jesus offered from the beginning.

enough

I am no expert in the Bible and its theology or history, but I have a knowing in my heart that I cannot explain, which no one can take away from me.

As I navigated having an active, busy toddler and a baby catching up to him, I spent every moment I could reframing my mind. I listened to podcasts and teachings, aiming to override and replace the junk in my mind. Chris and I kept peace, and I didn't talk openly about my faith discoveries or learnings. It was an inside job that needed to happen before I could confidently share what I was experiencing. I listened to a lot of music, which began to heal my soul at another level.

It was a hard time in our marriage. I think, like anyone in those early parenting days, so many unstable emotions and resentments form as well as outright confusion. My husband and I became further apart because of the demands and needs of these little people taking up residency in our lives. Chris would have his own story to tell, and it would be completely different to what I was experiencing.

My mind was messed up enough without adding to the mix the idea of not continuing my partnership with my absolute rock and best friend. We did, at one stage, discuss options for how I could receive some Centrelink payments for support and to move out but somehow keep the kids in touch with both of us. This completely devastated me. The only thing I could do at that moment was cry out to God in prayer.

'God, please help. I can't do this. We need to stay together. I'm sorry for all the things I have done up to this point. I want to be a better, loving, honouring, honest wife and mother. This is my greatest desire. I can't do this without Chris. Please help.'

I'm So Exhausted From the Fight

I didn't know if my prayer would work, but I literally had no other option. Quitting was not an option. Walking away was not an option. I couldn't stand the thought of the pain and suffering that journey would be. Of all the pain and suffering I had already faced within myself, I figured the hard thing of restoring our marriage had to be worth it. This I was willing to fight for, but I knew I was pretty shaky on the fight ground. I had a pretty poor track record of winning fights. Deep down I believed that I didn't deserve to win, so I wouldn't put in the effort.

My fight plan this time was rooted in love, and I knew who could provide all of the love I needed (and **more**). So, I stayed holding on to God, knowing and hoping that He could handle more of my junk than Chris could and realising that Chris didn't have to carry my junk. I could take it to God and not burden Chris with it. This had to take some of the pressure off him as a husband.

I didn't ever intentionally go out of my way to hurt Chris. I don't think anyone who is broken and hurting ever intends on hurting those they love with their actions and behaviours, but the reality is we do. Hurting people hurt people. If I was not going to address my own pain and step into healing and uncovering what was really going on inside, we never would have survived.

I decided to express love in every moment. If love meant keeping quiet about my feelings, I would keep quiet. If love meant speaking up, I would find the courage to express myself. This was such an unusual thing for me (and us), as I had kept quiet for so long and not been openly truthful to myself or Chris.

enough

There were some really tense moments where both of us would be abrupt and short in responding to the other person. My go-to was forgiveness. I forgave Chris. I forgave myself. That forgiveness freed me in each moment. That forgiveness offered peace and a new beginning as I began to let go of trying to control how things turned out and have everything perfect. My life was not perfect. I proved that the strategy of trying to be perfect was very far from effective, so this was worth a try.

The kids were probably what kept us civilised in most situations. Although there were challenges in terms of typical toddler behaviour and navigating the unknowns of parenting, we had nowhere else to go. Neither of us could escape and go on benders with our friends. We both suffered apart but together.

My bingeing and throwing up intensified, as I still continued not regulating my emotions. My faith was growing in my heart and my 'being' was being transformed, but my mind was still conditioned to these default patterns. I had tried and failed so many times in the past to begin again; I honestly thought that every new day was going to be the day that I would get it right.

At night, as I went to bed I was drained physically, mentally and emotionally, and I desperately wanted to get it right so I could feel good. It had been so long since I felt good, I forgot what that was like. This state of being took over me again. The 20 months or so of not repeating this behaviour while I was pregnant and nursing George was a blurry, fading memory.

It was such a tug of war between what I said I wanted and what I leaned towards in action. I couldn't fight any more. I can

I'm So Exhausted From the Fight

see now that each time I gave in to a temptation was because I was exhausted from the effort to resist and avoid and divert my mind from wanting to do that. Having the sugar fix and giving in to the temptation ended the struggle (for a moment) but then layered on me more guilt, shame and condemnation I was so used to.

Having God in the picture made me feel like I was letting God down as well. I wanted to believe that He was for me and created me amazing, wonderful, unique and all of the things I was hearing, but I just didn't let it sink in. My mind still believed the lies were my truth.

If I had known that the sugar cravings were an emotional void (not just a physical desire), I would have reached my cure a lot quicker. I even thought that God would cure me. I had heard stories of people being healed instantly from their disorder. Why can't that happen for me?

The struggle was still rooted in my mind. Neural pathways were set up on autopilot to drive my behaviours and keep me stuck. If I had fully known and understood the power I had to change and reset these pathways, life would have been a lot easier a lot sooner.

This is easy to look back on now and resolve that I could have done this or I could have tried that, and it all would have been fabulous. But I happened to experience what I did, and there is no condemnation in not knowing what you don't know.

I prayed prayers that were full truth and an acceleration to my wholeness. I read and researched materials that had the answers to what I was looking for. I dove deep into finding

out how the body and brain work, what our positive thoughts can do, how negative thoughts keep us stuck and how our feelings drive our thoughts.

My problem at this point was still a lot of pride in my way, expecting that I should be able to do it on my own and sort it out and redeem all of the mess. I was also spending a lot of time learning and understanding things but not putting into action the things that I knew. I was continually collecting information, ready for the 'one day' when I was ready to take faith-fuelled action. I was stuck in this state of fixed mindset conditioning. I tried every day to remain positive, overrule the negative default setting and press on to a better life, but every day the default was too strong. I would resort to a binge and throw up, and be left feeling useless again. I kept on the Herbalife shakes and supplements, knowing they helped me stay a little bit nourished around my lack of food intake.

I was completely exhausted from the fight. I could not go on, but I had subsequent thoughts that giving up was not an option, so I got up. Every day I tried to dream of a better life. My life was amazing, actually. The only thing to complain about was the issues I was creating myself. I noticed that whenever there was nothing hard going on, I would somehow make it hard. Injecting suffering onto myself reaffirmed the lie that I wasn't good enough.

Have you ever found yourself in a loop of self-sabotage, unable to escape its grip? My sabotaging behaviour was mindless eating that stemmed from an emptiness or void masked as unsatisfied hunger.

I'm So Exhausted From the Fight

I still questioned why I remained in this pattern. I'd get these cravings or hunger that, if I mindlessly tried to fill, were never satisfied, then I would adopt an attitude of 'I don't even care anymore' and spiral out of control.

If any normal person is hungry and eats the thing they're craving, they're good, right? If they overdo it, they end up feeling sick, don't they?

Not me, I'm not normal. **This** is not normal. I seriously can eat and eat and eat and eat and never be satisfied and not even feel too full or overindulged until it's too late. It's like those natural built-in systems that tell me 'You're full now' are broken or overwritten. I could go as far as to say it's like I'm possessed (again, like that drug addict looking for the next hit).

Now, that might be a little heavy, **but** seriously, ask anyone with an addiction what it's like to 'seek their hit' – nothing else will get in your way, nothing will satisfy, no one can convince you that you don't need it, and you won't stop until something gives. For me, the further I got into my condition, it's the guilt that gave – the realisation that **this** is **not,** in fact, helpful or kind to me. It's not serving me at all, and it is certainly not helpful to my family, who will be most impacted by the consequences of my sugar comedown or detox in the days following.

This. Is. Not. How. I. Want. To. Live.

This. Is. Not. Who. I. Want. To. Be.

This. Is. Not. Who. I. Am.

enough

And here I go again, seeking to find who I am, how I really want to live and all the ways I can make that possible by doing this and doing that and changing all these things and clearing my record and having a perfect streak of days, then weeks, then months of blissful healthy living, which in turn positions me on this cloud of healthy, happy living full of self-love and peace.

I thought this was not ever going to happen.

I claimed to be sorry. If I had this version of me envisioned in my head as a someday reality, I believed she **does not exist**.

This story is not about how I cleaned my life up and finally started living this wholesome, nourishing, blissful life to lead our children into guided 'love thyself' living. **Not true**. Not here. I cannot guarantee that for you. I cannot deliver that for you. This is a real struggle, and it's too big for me to overcome. When I was finally OK with accepting that as truth, I found relief and rested in my freedom.

All I can do to offer hope is share my surrender and encourage you in victory with reminders of the power behind choosing to believe the truth rather than the lies.

This journal entry jumps forward a fair bit in time, but it reflects what I was going through in 2012 and continued throughout – right into 2021.

I'm So Exhausted From the Fight

Journal Entry: 1 July 2021

I am so exhausted from the fight. I've been here a thousand times before. I'm tired a thousand times more. I should be past this by now. I know the strategies, I know the routine, I understand there are triggers and, in every moment, (**any moment**) I have a choice. Yet over and over again I choose … death, destruction, debilitating self-sabotage and painstaking regret, shame, dishonour.

When the advice is honour your bodies as a living sacrifice, I kill mine. One overloaded mouthful at a time. The craving at the forefront of my imagination playing full out.

In this moment I am disregarding all the truths I know and instead I believe the lie. YOU NEED THIS [insert sweet indulgent food]. You cannot concentrate or focus or go on until you end the suspense and just have the [insert sweet indulgent food] thing.

Again, I am defeated. Wounded. Worn out. Tired from the struggle. Drained from the war inside. I'm physically spent and emotionally bankrupt. I cannot go back and change what just happened. Once again, I live out the consequences. My heart bogs with regret and pity, wishing and hoping that this time is the last time. Yet, I fear my human weakness. The reality that I will repeat my own same past mistakes. I fear that I will not change. And my fear cripples me into not being able to change.

enough

Knowing that I've done this. I know what I'm doing. I know how not to do it. But I continue to foolishly go there and end up here.

In the pit.

Seeing myself standing victorious seems such a distant, unreachable ambition. It seems so far away from where I stand. In this moment I mourn for that victory. I mourn for the chance to do it over and make a different choice.

I resolve the definition of insanity is doing the same thing over and over again and expecting different results – thanks Albert Einstein, you rock.

I don't want to be insane anymore.

I don't want to do the same thing over and over again.

I want different results.

I've had enough.

Definition of **Enough**[1]

pronoun

1 As much or as many of something as required.

---

[1] Enough. In: *Dictionary.com*, https://www.lexico.com/definition/Enough.

I'm So Exhausted From the Fight

'you need to get enough of the right things to eat'

1.1 Used to indicate that one is unwilling to tolerate any more of something undesirable.

'I've had enough of this behaviour'

Phrases

enough said

There is no need to say more; all is understood.

enough is enough

No more will be tolerated.

'someone has got to stand up and say enough is enough'

enough is as good as a feast

proverb

Moderation is more satisfying than excess.

I thought this fight was over. Enough. I've done enough. I've been through enough (put myself through enough). I can't fight anymore. Enough.

I'm done.

enough

When I reach for the sweetness after a meal, I remind myself, 'That's enough. You've had enough. There is no need for any more food. You're done.'

Yet, whenever that condemning voice came in, I wanted it more. When I offered grace and love and a way out towards living the hope-filled life I wanted, I could stop there. It took me a long time to work out this approach and the difference between when I was harsh on myself and when I was kind.

Self-talk matters.

I cannot emphasise enough the importance of becoming aware of your self-talk. My default chatter and conditioning was a bully like no other, and I know I am not the only one who struggles with this self-doubting, condemning, nagging voice inside that just won't let up.

I discovered affirmations and tried to apply positive words to offer myself a rewiring, but many of them felt fake. I still had trouble believing good about myself. As I explored more of the inner work and went through the process of deeper soul searching, I began to find that taking action on the belief I was trying to embody was more powerful than just saying it and trying to renew my mind from the top-down. I had to embrace these truths from the heart out, which meant getting myself to **feel** the feelings and then declare their truth and act as if it was true.

It matters how we talk to ourselves. Be kind. Consider how you are feeling. Affirm the truth and then act accordingly – say things like 'I am fully known and fully loved, and I am enough', then engage with others from that position. Be honest and open with them. Most of all, be kind. Treat yourself that way.

When I discovered that surrender didn't mean giving up and giving in and being a victim but meant standing in the victory that is already won and claiming the freedom I already have, I could stop fighting.

This was never my fight to win. I am already a winner.

> **Journal entry: 5 March 2022**
>
> The only way you're going to get out of this addiction is if you replace it with something stronger.
>
> Replace the habit with something stronger and more fulfilling than the thing you crave right now.
>
> The importance of living without walls up. Walls block out those who love us. Walls prevent us from walking freely. Walls stop us from moving forward, reaching our destiny.
>
> Tear down your walls brick by brick. Stop placing your hope in that which can never truly protect you.
>
> May you be fully known and fully loved right where you are. Yes. In your mess. In your bad habits. In the prison you have built for yourself. One brick today.

enough

> You don't need to have it all sorted and packed up and rubble cleared away in order to heal and fully step into love. Remove just one brick and allow that love to flow over the gap you have created and into your heart.
>
> Your greatest weakness can be turned into your greatest strength.

When is it ever enough?

Is your burnt-out life glorifying the freedom you stand for? We live in a world that congratulates the hustle and striving and forever-reaching for more culture. But when is it ever enough?

I sort the clothes, wipe the benches and pack away the belongings. I'll rearrange this space, then sort through those things, take care of that, then peg the washing, prepare more food, pack away the mess, wipe the benches, move those things, deal with that, more, more, more – always more to do. But when will I sit and relax? When will I do that passion project my heart yearns for? When is everything ever accomplished fully so that I can rest?

It's not.

When it's never enough, we need to step back into the position of knowing that we are enough. Without all the doing and all the things. Without the ticked-off to-do list and accomplished titles. We are enough – right here, right now.

I have enough, I do enough, I am enough. I let go of the burden of feeling like I need to do more. I am always enough. I can't emphasise that enough. I want you to really sink into the wholehearted truth of accepting you **are** enough.

It's not about the clothes you wear, food you eat, shops you shop at or who you associate with. It's not any of those things. Nothing out there can define the wholesome goodness of what's **in** there – in the depths of your soul, at the core of your being. Once upon a time, you were born and in that very moment, for the entirety of your life, **who** you are is enough. Isn't that cool?

Body fact: Enough pressure on the digestive system

I am no expert in this, but once I became aware of the science and function of our digestive system and how it serves our body, I began to realise the implications my eating habits were having on my whole body, including my emotional state, which was what began driving this disorder in the first place.

You can do your own research, and I encourage you to, because I'm not going to cover the intricacies of all that I have learnt, but I will share how it has helped me continue to recover and heal. This can help anyone who struggles with food in any sense, anyone who tends to have cravings or snack ineffectively or find they are overeating and suffering because of it.

Only recently have I discovered the power of fasting, and although this is not a great recommendation for anyone who has struggled with abstaining from food, at this point in my healing the science made sense and I had enough wisdom

enough

to lean into the benefits of letting our digestive system have a break, even simple things like leaving enough break time between eating.

There were days throughout my journey when I would literally be consuming something **all** day long. All day, something was going in my mouth (and therefore into my system for my body to process). If I stuffed in enough during a binge, I would get rid of most of it during the vomiting. But man, oh man, how damaging this was to my organs and gut health and body function – not to mention the dehydration, headaches, malnourishment, chemical imbalances and hormone fluctuations.

All of that knowledge now can play as power. We've all heard that knowledge is power, but I had the knowledge and knew what to do, so I would go even further to say that knowledge and awareness backed by intentional action is a superpower.

CHAPTER 7

The Unseen Battle and Warfare

Strong when I am weak.

Yesterday was 1 January 2015. The beginning of a new year. A day for reflection and planning. A day of rest and 'quiet play' as my husband slept off his NYE hangover. Yesterday was the day I made a decision. A firm decision. Now, don't be alarmed, I've done this before (made a decision), and generally when I stick with my decision and apply commitment and discipline, I see results beyond anything I could have imagined. It's not rocket science; just a basic life principle.

enough

Want to know what my decision is?

I'll tell you anyway – Yesterday, I decided that I am going to give up processed sugar. Indefinitely.

I have successfully done this before (from November to February, two years ago), and since then I've attempted and failed many times to do it again.

What's saying I won't fail again this time? This time, I'm not relying on my own strength.

OK, why give up sugar? Why not just enjoy it in moderation, like the food pyramid suggests?

Because my weakness is sugar. And when I am weak and I have sugar, I fall into the temptation to binge, uncontrollably overload myself and feel absolutely rotten on the inside and out. I'm sick of treating myself like this and being a victim of my own actions, so I'm taking a stand. It actually triggers something uncontrollable in me, and I can't fight the fight anymore.

Today was 'day one'. How did it go?

Well, I feel good. I was busy and active. I ate a lot of fruit and kept my theme of eating relatively sweet (only because I've been consuming so many sweets lately, I know that I have to ease myself into the whole change). Breakfast was porridge (nothing added) and a fresh juice (pineapple, apple, kiwi fruit, lemon and water). I snacked on a piece of roast meat and cheese while cooking the kids' toasted sandwiches. For lunch, I made two slices of French toast with blueberries, banana, cinnamon and pure maple syrup with a glass of milk, then some almonds and cashews. Midafternoon, I had a handful of choc-coated blueberries (healthy) and a bite of the kids' apple. Dinner was meat and veg, then half a nectarine. I didn't have any super cravings, nor did I feel tempted by the leftover supply of chocolates or sweets that are stashed in the fridge. I know it's going to be totally different tomorrow and the next day after that. I am simply taking it one day at a time and trying to stay as in tune with my body (and soul) as possible.

Why are there even leftover chocolates and sweets in the house, you ask?!?

Because I wanted to really test myself. I wanted to be able to face the challenge with obstacles and overcome them anyway. I want to conquer. It's not a test of knowledge if you have all the answers at your fingertips, is it? It's not a competitive game if you have no opposition, is it? It's not a victory if you have no adversary. It's not a test of strength if you have no resistance. This is my way of not taking the easy way out. I know it's going to be hard. Let's be real. Probably even harder than the first time I did it, and possibly even harder than every time I tried after that (and failed).

I am a strong believer in the Bible and the truths within its pages. I have had personal experiences on a spiritual level that have proven to me the power of God. I want to share this with others so that there is no misconception that I am some kind of superwoman or self-made success story. I do not possess great power within me or generate willpower from the depths of my being apart from God. When I am weak, He is my strength to draw from. I am a new creation (as it states in 2 Corinthians 5:17 – 'Therefore, if anyone is in Christ, he is a new creation; old things have passed away; behold, all things have become new').

My old self was bulimic. I underwent no counselling or medication to overcome the condition after exhausting all attempts on my own to 'get better' and 'be healed'. I resorted only to throw myself into the depths of the Word and search for answers in the Bible. In March 2012 I became a Christian, and I thank God for every revelation I receive and the process of sanctification I have been on since.

I believe … (and this is what's going to get me through the next two days, 30 days and 365 days to follow).

When I am feeling weak, there is always Grace.

2 Corinthians 12:9–10 – 'But he said to me, "My grace is sufficient for you, for my power is made perfect in weakness." Therefore, I will boast all the more gladly about my weaknesses so that Christ's power may rest on me. That is why, for Christ's sake, I delight in weaknesses, in insults, in hardships, in persecutions, in difficulties. For when I am weak, then I am strong.'

> I'm so grateful. When I'm grateful (rather than resentful at my humanness), the atmosphere changes. I change. My position immediately becomes a place of victory through no power of my own other than the decision to surrender and let go.
>
> 1 Corinthians 15:57 – 'But thanks be to God, who gives us the victory through our Lord Jesus Christ.'

Even with faith, I went through these patterns of up–down–up–down–up–up–up–down–down–up. I constantly fell back down when I strived on my own strength. I'm sure I heard many, many times along the way the power of renewing my mind, the beauty in surrendering and all of the things I am pointing you towards here. But I had to **get it** for myself before I fully grasped the intensity of what I was learning. It took action.

If you have lessons you need to learn, be kind to yourself. Don't be hard. We're all doing this journey blind. **No one** really knows how it's all going to play out. When you stay surrendered and open to the possibility of not having it all together and not being fully in control, you position yourself for grace – undeserved, unmerited favour – and that is humbling.

I **know** how much I don't deserve the love that is poured out on me. I **know** all of my deepest, darkest secrets and inadequacies, but so does the **One** who created me and yet **He loves me** unconditionally and **He loves you** with that same tenacious unconditional, never–giving–up–on–you kind of love. I know because I've been there. I've run for so

enough

long into other things that offer me hope, and they were all empty promises. I **know** God is faithful. He is the reason this book is being orchestrated. He is the reason certain people are in my life, and I get to share His love in a way that is not condemning or rule–binding or religious.

It's real. Tangible.

It's **enough**.

God's love is enough.

Jesus is enough.

You are enough.

In February 2013, we moved from Dolgelly to a property called Warrabri, 90 kilometres north–west of Goondiwindi. Chris and I were in a much better place, and the job Chris was entering was with a family–run farming enterprise, which he slotted into like another brother. The owners lived on their main property, south of Goondiwindi, and we were the only ones living at Warrabri. This was another hour away from our family down south.

Our new home was a pokey little cottage and needed quite a lot of yard work compared to the lovely homestead–style place we just left. But that wasn't important to us. What was important to me was that we were still together and still close to Goondiwindi, where I had made so many connections and friends. Not really anybody knew the struggles that we went through, and that is probably another book on its own. I had settled my eating enough to be only sporadic, occasional relapses, and I seemed to be doing better more than I was doing worse.

By 2015, we waited for the arrival of our third baby, Kate.

Over the years, as I grew in my faith and understanding of God, I could talk about my struggle like it was a past thing, but I knew it was still there and would still rear its ugly head when I was not expecting it. I gradually became more self-aware and could implement strategies I'd learned along the way to avoid derailing.

I developed a greater understanding of the things we can't see, as in spiritual warfare and things that our human brain can't explain. This insight created more growth and freedom and more depth in my faith journey. People I know who share my faith can attest that I love to talk about it. I am so curious and lit up by the intricacies of life and figuring out why we are all here, lining up with that and then living it out!

I had gone back to some regular work over the years of George and Claire being little, which gradually loosened the strain of the financial pressure that hit us in 2012. This also provided me with mental stimulation, which activated parts of my brain that were otherwise stagnant. I think all of the mothers know what I'm talking about here. The distraction from the needs of your family and the chance to challenge another part of your brain can deliver the same benefits as having a retreat from parenting to get a massage or have someone clean your house.

I needed the balance of being a mum and going to work in order to not slip back into the old anxious patterns that hit me before. Maybe this was another unhealthy way to distract

enough

myself without facing the depths of my internal trauma and reaching full healing, but it worked for a time. Running to work and being too busy to get too deep and self-developed meant I couldn't do the deep work. I think this is a bit of a trap we all face in society – it's easier to get busy and distracted than to go into doing the hard inner work.

There was a lot of inner work that needed doing. I have since realised that there will always be inner work to do as I continue to grow and reach for all that is available to me. To reach my full potential, I need to keep moving the needle forward. I will forever keep growing.

It is a battle and a war, and if we relax and let our guard down, we can become a victim in an instant. I have experienced this so much. The positioning of my heart and mind are crucial to the success of my victory. It took me a long time to realise that it is in **all** three aspects of our being that we find wholeness (even in the brokenness). I had learned about mind, body and soul. I'd seen all of these things that promise to keep you in perfect peace – like holistic healing and all of those things – but it wasn't until I fully understood that this is how God planned it from the beginning that I realised the truth I had access to was what the world was trying to tell me all along. Knowing this helped me to get to this place of being brave enough to share my story and walk openly in my faith.

Chris had softened toward my faith over the years as I continued to go to Bible study and be part of the faith community without turning into a complete weirdo (I guess! I'm not too sure he would fully agree here, but I'll leave it at that). I certainly was a different person from the binge drinking, dancing-on-the-bar partygoer I was in our early dating and married life, but I think kids do that to you anyway, in a sense. I appreciate a cup of tea and a good podcast while ironing and an early night in over going out to drink endless amounts of alcohol and dancing like a rockstar. It's my age and maturity more than my weird faith, right?

Either way, we went through the years living on this property we could treat like our own, raising our three beautiful children. George and Claire went off to kindy and then school in our little community at Toobeah and Kioma, followed by Kate in 2018. These years were so precious and so full of memories, I find myself blotting out most of the difficulties of being so far out of town, not having close family around and trying to juggle work and kids. It just became life. It's all that we knew, and all that we know still. We've had to do it together and get stronger at doing it together because there is no other option.

I was constantly listening to faith-building audio, whether it was music, stories, podcasts, radio interviews or church sermons. Whenever I have the chance I (still to this day) would feed my mind with truth. Any slip of neglecting to do that would present in me a struggle and fight that I knew I didn't want to go back to – a struggle that I knew I couldn't fight. So, while there were occasions where I would still struggle with my eating, I knew where to run and was getting better at surrendering to love. I was taking better care of myself physically as well as mentally and now emotionally.

We lived at Warrabri until 2023. In 2020, Kate started school at our small bush school in Kioma, following George and Claire. Then, the world shut down due to coronavirus, and

enough

we homeschooled for a little. But, as George was entering Year 6 the following year and we were looking at high school options, we made the decision to transition all three kids into a larger, but still small, Christian College in Goondiwindi to get him socially ready. The distance to the bus was 40 kilometres. It was 86 kilometres to town, so instead of doing an 80–kilometre round trip each morning and afternoon and long trips on the bus, we decided I would drive them to school and work three days a week as a teacher aide.

The move into a Christian environment was massive, given Chris's resistance and hesitancy at the start of my faith journey, but I believe this is a testament to the softening of his heart and change in atmosphere that came with me staying close to God and trusting. God is not giving up on us. Also, note here that the enemy is not giving up. There are many internal struggles that happen throughout our life that express another form of unseen battle and warfare.

> **Journal Entry: Enough with the torment**
>
> I claimed on a Tuesday night Zoom call in 2022 that I am going to write my book. It is finished, I am an author, it is what is going to propel my impact and bring glory to God (because this isn't about me).
>
> **23 May 2023** – The statement that changed my life from a therapist I heard on the Mel Robbins Podcast: 'I want to help the part of you that wants healing, wants wellness, wants to be whole.'

That was it, there was part of me that wanted help, wanted to get better, wanted healing and wholeness and all of the goodness and blessings that were being poured out into my life, but there was a destructive part of me that was preventing me from experiencing that fully, and I couldn't work out why.

There **is** a part of me that wants to be healed. Whole. On purpose. She's there. I've just let this other scared, protective part of me keep me from the pain of stepping out of my comfort zone. The process of growth and nurturing I have been on over the last 12 months has been so revolutionary to my whole being. I guess taking the perspective that this is part of a bigger picture and the story isn't over yet, gives me space to **be** right where I am, and be OK with the shortcomings and difficult things I've cultivated. The reality is the patterns in my mind and brain have been created over time. There is a time it takes to override, rewire and take back the ground that I've 'lost' in the sense of the years I spent in inner turmoil.

This podcast episode, along with another discussion about 'perfectly hidden depression', helped me realise that these things I was struggling with were **not** uncommon, and it was not untreatable. Hope just got more real. Hope that I can be fully free and not just managing and keeping my condition under control.

All this time I have simply wanted to melt into that place of pure love and just be held in absolute, unconditional, never-ending, as–deep–as–you–can–begin–to–imagine love.

And all the time it's been there. I've just been resistant to receiving because my programming has me believing that I am not worthy of that love.

My mind lines up with the truth now and I **know** without a doubt that love is available, that love has been calling me, that love is never leaving me, and that love is deserving of my surrender to it. I cannot resist any more. I cannot hold it back, block it off or stop it from consuming me.

Like a consuming fire, there is no way I can escape God's love. And there is no reason I should have to. He created me **in his image. He is love**. I am a reflection of God's love. When I stain myself with low self-esteem, low self-worth and destructive behaviour, I am denying the world from knowing His love. I am hurting myself. I am hurting those who love me, and I am hurting the ones He is trying to reveal himself to. Most importantly and significantly, I am hurting God. His heart hurts when I don't walk in my authority and true identity. I am not honouring my Creator when I live small and play small, I am glorifying the enemy and fulfilling his plan to steal, kill and destroy.

Ooof. I'll take that as a confronting truth.

The truth can sometimes hurt, but maybe it's that growth pain we need to break away from where we are stuck and actually position ourselves to flourish.

We were not born to be hidden.

We were not saved to be in a safe place on the mantlepiece.

We were saved so that we could be set free and live an abundant life!

We're called to show the world what is available when you put your faith in Jesus.

If we are not living that, then we are not living true to our purpose and God-given potential.

With Him and **through** Him, **all things** are possible. All things.

If you are living with limitations right now, then I would say you're not fully aligned with the truth that has set you free.

Because freedom has no limits.

Think about that. True freedom has no limits.

Be true to yourself. Be fully authentic with the world, especially those close to you.

enough

Why are we limiting God?

In May 2022, I purchased an Enagic Water Ionisor – a Japanese medical– grade device that produces Kangen Water® – through a friend offering a business opportunity to share my passion for health and wellness. Over the years, I have explored similar ventures in the multi–level network marketing world where we fall in love with a product and share it with people whom we think it could benefit and earn commissions in the process. This concept wasn't new to me, and while it is a very rewarding business model, my past experiences with overwhelming self–doubt and destructive habits left me questioning whether I could succeed at this.

Kangen Water® is the name of alkaline drinking water created through an electrolysis process using the water ioniser, and it has three unique properties that make it special: It is alkaline, has strong antioxidant properties and is rich in hydrogen and minerals.

After thoroughly researching the product and the science behind how it helps our bodies heal and function optimally, I figured, 'What have I got to lose?'. If it could support the current health and healing I had been attempting so far, then it was worth giving a go.

Enagic, founded in 1974, has a long–established reputation, yet I'm still amazed by how little education there is about hydration and the different types of water in the Western world.

I was beginning to fully understand the damage I did to my body and experience the long–term effects of being in that state for such a long period. I understood that hydration is exactly the foundation to life. So, whenever I had all these other things going on – like eating whole foods, reducing sugars and processed foods, taking supplements and exercising regularly – if I didn't have good hydration to support me, I was basically wasting my time, energy and effort on all of these other things. It just made sense.

I did still have a deep but distant (back there in the past somewhere) desire to earn extra income from home, and while I didn't believe I could do it because I'd messed it up so many times, there was an offer to participate in weekly MindGym sessions which helped us to show up, do the work and dig deeper into our personal growth and development. I realised how much I had been placing limits on my faith through wrong thinking patterns.

I had never taken this much action before. Being someone who relied heavily on doing it myself and working it out alone, I often retreated from group momentum communities like this. If I was going to let anyone down, I wanted it to be me and me only. I didn't want to disappoint or let down someone else who was relying on me. I think this is why I never truly took any further steps towards leadership because there would be people counting on me, and I couldn't handle the responsibility. With this experience of uncovering my limiting beliefs and truly seeking what I believed to be true, I encountered my strengths in a whole new way and, as a result, also deepened my conviction of faith and trust in God.

As well as our family's health improving, my vision for what this business vehicle could create for us began to take flight. A few of the women I was working with organised a team retreat in October 2023, and this is when I grabbed hold of

enough

the heart-centred approach to the life I am living now. Like I said, I knew the headwork and could get all of the theory, but I never attuned myself to listen to how my body was responding to situations and what my emotions were telling me, which kept me stuck in that cycle and pattern for so long.

October was the time that I connected with the publishing company and put a date on my book. There was a lot that flowed out of those four days away, and getting fully aligned was one of them.

From the retreat, there was an opportunity to join a community of women in a six-week program called the Aligned Woman Academy. While this doesn't hold all of my Christian beliefs, I trusted the process would reveal more of my misalignment and get me on track with my faith where I was lacking a kind of oneness.

We had a small group exercise on the last day of the retreat, exploring the environment and collecting items on a treasure hunt-style adventure. As I and three other women sat on the beach and reflected on our experience, I shared the title of my book and the overview of my journey. Out of that conversation, we noted down our meaningful words from the retreat:

Surrender.

Sisterhood.

Growth.

Enough.

The Unseen Battle and Warfare

My reflections when I returned home were so eye-opening. Understanding that we are at war but don't fight alone, I know there is more of an unseen battle than we can comprehend.

I was comforted by these words – 'As the flaming arrows fly at you, God will protect you. You don't have to be afraid.'

'He will cover you with his feathers, and under his wings you will find refuge; his faithfulness will be your shield and rampart.' – Psalm 91:4

'In addition to all this, take up the shield of faith, with which you can extinguish all the flaming arrows of the evil one.' – Ephesians 6:16

> **I think we miss the feelings too often.**
>
> 3:44 am, Friday, 10 May 2024
>
> You look amazing. You look sick. You look worried, stressed, anxious. You look great. You look like you need a feed. You look like you've eaten too much. You look hungry.
>
> How about, 'How are you feeling?'!
>
> I'm not saying we should only listen and obey our feelings. I'm not. Sometimes they are very out of line with the truth, but our feelings are a feedback mechanism. They offer us feedback on what's going on

either physically, mentally, emotionally or all three. We have to take that feedback for what it is and question it.

What are you trying to tell me?

What is it that I need to know here?

What can I do with where I'm at?

Does it feel good?

Does it feel right?

Is this in alignment with **who** I truly am on the inside?

Does it reflect the truth?

Because if it doesn't, we need to address that. Otherwise, the feeling is going to control and dictate what happens next, and often if we are operating on autopilot and not being conscious or aware of our feelings (feedback system), then we will default into survival mode because that is one of our basic human needs to feel safe, secure, loved and out of danger.

If our feelings or instincts trigger any kind of risk of danger, our emotions respond in reaction mode. Our goal is to survive and regulate our nervous system (and our body/being) back to safety.

If we regulate our feelings and continue to come back into awareness of them, we can get to that place of knowing we are safe, secure, loved and OK – out of danger. And we can live our lives accordingly from a place of fulfilment and wholeness, not lack or emptiness.

Let's sit with that for a moment.

CHAPTER 8

You are NOT a Victim

Let's talk about parenting. I don't, for one second, blame my dad or my mum for the onset of my condition. I think there was a lot of perfectionism inside of me that was not caused by any outside pressure or expectation from anyone else; it was just the way I was wired and the thought patterns and scripts I let run wild in my head. Maybe at some stage I held blame that 'Oh, nothing was ever right. I was always told I was wrong. They expected me to be perfect and never make mistakes and always look like I was doing it better than everyone else.'

Well, maybe a little bit of that expectation was there. And I don't judge them for having high expectations of me. Of course, we want our kids to be their best and do their best.

enough

I had such a fixed mindset that led me to interpret those interactions as 'If I don't get this right, I'm doomed. I'm done for. There is no redemption. I'm out. The end.' This can be referred to in the world as a fixed mindset.

There was a lot of out-of-proportion thinking during that time, but I never recognised it. I never told anyone what I was struggling with, and I was so good at hiding it so that no one ever entered my space and asked the right questions.

With the amount of inner work and mindset shifting I've done, especially these last few years, I have really been able to excavate the rubbish and identify what was going on at that time. Because of this, I'm able to go back – through my memories, through my experiences – and basically 'parent' myself in the way that I needed at the time. The scared little girl inside me needed some encouragement, grace, self-confidence and courage. She wasn't getting it from herself; it had to be planted and nurtured, but nobody realised it was missing. This little girl needed guidance on how to discard the old, toxic, unhelpful thought patterns and replace them with healthier ones.

Again, not blaming or pointing fingers at my parents for the role they played or the job they did at raising me, but with so much self-awareness (and the knowledge and power of God that I have now), I'm able to visit that time with love and nurture and be guided through what was such a confusing and tormenting time (inside me!) I'm discovering that God can heal our inner being if we invite Him in to do it.

The battle within was raging, and no one could see. No one would have ever known. This is soooo common. Maybe they did know and just felt so unequipped and unqualified, they didn't know what to say or how to address it.

What my hope here in this chapter is to be able to equip parents (and those suffering or struggling) to start that conversation, have those moments of reflection and really shine a light into the darkness, because the longer you leave things in the shadows, they can multiply and feel too overwhelming, too consuming.

My parents did the best they could with what they knew. And I believe, if you are a parent, you too are doing the best you can with what you know. If you have parents, trust me, they are doing the best they can with what they know.

There's soooo much we don't know; we need to acknowledge that. We don't know everything, and that is OK. We don't need to know everything. All we need to know is the next right thing. What can I do with this? Who can I be from here on in? What can I do from here, in this moment?

The most powerful answer is love.

I can love unconditionally.

I can love into the next action step.

Blaming other people or situations keeps you stuck. For a long time, I did blame my parents and held on to their shortcomings, and it kept me captive as a victim. Poor me. The only way to true freedom is to own **all** of you. Take full responsibility and have radical acceptance for **everything**. Only then can you take the necessary steps to heal, overcome and rewrite or

enough

rewire your conditioning to obtain the outcome you desire or are destined for.

This is not woo-woo manifesting, like you just have to hope and dream and imagine and it will become reality. This is human physiology. Science. Nature. Creation. It's how we were created and designed.

When we line up with how we are meant to be living, when we are truthful and honest and authentic, then we can live fully. (Who doesn't want a bit more of that in the world?!) We can live freely – free from guilt, shame and trapped patterns and habits.

Let's ignite honesty and transparency. Bring it all into the light. Shine the light. If there is any darkness or secrets or hidden things, it will destroy your soul. Let it out now.

You are beautiful.

You are loved.

You are made in the image of God (God is love).

Everything about you was perfectly and intricately designed to be **you** – unique, wonderful, amazing. Even the bits you don't like. Even the bits that don't reach your bar of perfection. Even your big hands or hairy arms or chunky knees (I've always hated mine). No one is obsessing over these things as much as you. And when you learn to accept and be grateful and so proud of who you are becoming as you journey through life with a heart full of love, you will realise **none** of us are perfect, not even the girl you admire (or envy) so much because she is **the best** at everything, has perfect features and is just so graceful and amazing. Even she is not perfect. She needs love and acceptance just like you.

Why can't I just get it together and stop this?

I had no idea it was an issue of identity. While I can see that now, I initially did not believe I was worthy. I did not believe I was loveable. I did not believe I was worth fighting for. So, I stayed a victim, beaten and bruised by my internal dialogue, and struggled for a span of more than 20 years.

At age 20, I vowed in the lead-up to our wedding that I would stop, that's it. It's over. It's done. That's enough. No more. Yet, I remained bound, hating on myself even more for failing to break free. I condemned and blamed myself for messing up again and again as I let myself down, let my husband down.

He had been on this roller coaster with me from the start, and he did everything he could to pour love and acceptance into me, although I remained hard and resistant, blocking it from affecting me on a heart level. Whenever I would come up for confession again, it was like placing a dagger straight into his heart. He didn't understand. **Why** would I keep behaving like this?

I also didn't understand **why** I was repeatedly behaving like this! I was consumed with the thought 'I must be really bad. I've really messed up now', and so I would layer on a heavier weight of burden.

enough

Enough. For the woman who has had enough of believing the lies. For the girl who is ready to come face to face with the truth that she is enough, right where she is. For the one ready for freedom and healing.

This is not about doing more. It's not a book on adding things to do that will improve your life or allow you to stride towards healing. It's a book about being.

We have enough to do already. I get it, you're busy. You can't change the things you're not coping with because they are how you autopilot your way through life in order to survive. That's OK. I've been there too, and I strived for **yeaarrrrs** trying to fix, mend, patch up, rebuild, overcome – all the things that require so much effort and energy – only to end up right back where I was. Feeling hopeless, helpless and wounded. Beaten beyond repair. **Every. Single. Time.** Weakened and unable to fight, I would plateau in my mess of destruction for a while until I was ready and feeling sick and tired enough to will myself to get back up and try again.

Determined. Yet defeated.

Willing. Yet unable.

Desperate. And afraid.

I would try, try again.

Do the thing, add the gratitude back in, use your journal, allow yourself to be quiet and still and present. Reset your body, reset your mind.

How long can we go on in this supercharged change-the-world-by-changing-your-life kind of state? However long you will allow it.

But let me just say this: One more day like that is too long. It's time now to be enough, without changing anything. Without setting an action plan in place or another to-do list. This moment is where you meet yourself in full surrender and declare enough.

This is where I came to in the journey of my faith, where I could be in the presence of my creator King and know that all of my flaws, all of my weaknesses, my mistakes and past struggles **don't define me**. What He says about me does, and that is enough.

This being aligns your thoughts and emotions with the reality of God's goodness in a world wrought with lies. Knowing your true identity breeds joy and trust rather than entitlement, negativity or uncertainty. There's a cultivating that takes place. These are seeds you are planting in your heart – tilling the soil, churning it over until it becomes receptive to the fullness of God and filled with the fruit of the spirit. Just sit with that for a moment.

I'm even going to say it again: These are seeds you are planting in your heart – tilling the soil, churning it over until it becomes receptive to the fullness of God and filled with the fruit of the spirit.

Claim the day.

Claim the moment.

enough

Claim your position.

Claim your freedom.

Breathe in life.

Be gone, worries.

Breathe in hope.

Be gone, struggle.

Breathe in love.

Be gone, fear.

Breathe in joy.

Be gone, helplessness.

Breathe in peace.

Be gone, every lie.

I'm not going to give you a declaration to start your day. Instead, I'm going to give you an exercise, which will position you to connect with your own powerful, heartfelt internal declaration. I hope you can stay with it long enough to feel it run through your body like your heartbeat and surrender to the unconditional love your soul craves.

The love that has a plan for you and loves you beyond anything you can think or imagine is available to you right now, fully expectant, open arms embracing you as you fall into grace.

OK, here is an exercise for you to try:

> **Crafting your own heartfelt declaration:**
>
> My best advice for getting the most out of this exercise is to record the following instructions as a voice note. This way, you can listen intently and be fully present in the moment. Feel free to pause between steps to write things down.
>
> 1. **Get comfortable**
>   Find a quiet, peaceful space where you can be still. Sit down, relax and close your eyes. Take several deep breaths in through your nose. As you breathe, allow any tension or worries to leave your body. You might even like to play a soothing song to settle you into the exercise.
>
> 2. **Reflect on where you are**
>   Gently reflect on your current state. What are the things you've been striving for? What burdens have you been carrying? What lies or limiting beliefs have held you back? Write them down, naming them honestly, without judgement.
>   - o Example prompts: (Only read these examples if you're feeling really stuck. I encourage you to start writing before reading ahead – you'll

be surprised at how much the answers are already within you, and you may not need these prompts to guide you.)
- "I've been telling myself I'm not good enough because …"
- "I've been carrying the weight of …"
- "I've been trying so hard to change because I feel …"

3. **Release**

   Take a moment to surrender these burdens. Picture yourself laying them down. Let go of the need to fix or change anything right now. Write down what you want to release, and speak these words of surrender aloud:
   - "I surrender … I release … I let go of the pressure to …"
   - Example: "I surrender my need for control. I let go of the belief that I have to be perfect to be worthy."

4. **Embrace grace**

   Now focus on receiving love and grace. Know that you are enough just as you are. Picture yourself being embraced by unconditional love. Allow your heart to be open to the truth that you are loved, worthy and whole.
   - Write down affirmations or truths you want to believe about yourself:
     - "I am enough."
     - "I am loved, even in my brokenness."
     - "I am worthy of joy and peace."

5. **Write your declaration**

   In this space of grace, write a heartfelt declaration of who you are, grounded in truth and love. Let it come from deep within you. It should reflect the freedom, love and worth that you know belong to you without striving.
   - Example template: "Today I declare that I am [fill in your truth]. I release the belief that I need to [let go of a lie]. I open my heart to receive [what you desire – love, peace, joy]. I trust that I am guided by [God, faith, love, grace]. I am enough."

6. **Claim it daily**

   As you finish writing your declaration, place your hand on your heart and read it aloud. Feel its truth resonate within you. I also like to record this in a voice note and listen daily.

   When you commit to speaking, listening to or reading this declaration every day, especially in moments when doubt arises, you will find your faith build, as you are reminded of the love and freedom that are already yours. This overriding with the truth will eliminate the lies you have been playing in your life on replay.

If you have trouble coming up with the positive, true aspects of your identity, what I have found to be helpful is to list down the current things you believe about yourself – negative, positive, destructive, helpful and all. Then, consider this list has been handed to you by someone you admire and adore so

enough

intensely, that as you begin to read it you can easily identify what is an absolute lie and replace it with truth. Replace it with **love** and **encouragement**. Remember, you are doing this for someone you care deeply for and want nothing but goodness in their life. That is how I want you to see yourself!

As much as I can understand that some people may not be there yet, because the years of hate and destruction and disgust are so long, when you love yourself back into truth, accepting that you are already loved (even though you know you're not perfect and not enough), you will find freedom from these lies. When you can receive love – pure, unconditional love that you don't deserve – you will begin to relate to yourself differently, and healing will continue. This is called grace.

To anyone who is suffering and struggling with any kind of unseen battle and warfare, I want you to know **you** are **not** a victim.

What's my practical strategy when I'm tempted? I know that faith isn't for everyone, but for me Jesus is my no-formula strategy. He meets me in my struggle.

Here's what that looks like practically:

First, I gently remind myself that this is not who I am anymore. I'm not someone who snacks after a meal. I declare that I savour the delicious nourishment I've just given my body and trust it will sustain and energise me abundantly. I give thanks and land in gratitude.

Next, I evaluate what's happening in my body that's making me feel like I 'want' this sweet indulgence. I ask myself:

What's the emotion behind this? Is there an unmet need I could address in another way? Is there a spiritual deficit that I'm trying to satisfy physically?

I take a moment to become present, stepping away from the survival state that spirals my mind towards destruction in a panic.

I breathe deeply.

I distance myself from the food and take notice of the thoughts bombarding me.

I calmly sort through them. This is where I meet Jesus. He is the unfailing peace in my storm, and I know I cannot calm it on my own.

I encourage you to find your own way to peace, whether through faith or another grounding practice that brings you back to yourself in moments of temptation and spiralling. There is no resolve in trying to get away from yourself. Believe me, I've tried this many times and failed.

Then after that, I reach for mint. I either take a mint – some peppermint gum or a hot water with peppermint essential oil – or brush my teeth. It seems to be enough to get me over the initial craving.

Finally, I hold onto a promise. In these moments, I often recall scripture that speaks directly to my heart, reminding me that I am an imperfect human and it's not wrong to feel this way or face temptation. This verse, in particular, brings me back to that truth:

enough

First Corinthians 10:13 (NIV): "No temptation has overtaken you except what is common to mankind. And God is faithful; He will not let you be tempted beyond what you can bear. But when you are tempted, He will also provide a way out so that you can endure it."

With that, I rest. I rest in my identity. I rest knowing that the feelings, emotions, anxiousness and turmoil will pass. I rest in the certainty that it will be OK. I will be OK. Another level of healing takes place.

CHAPTER 9

The Death of the Thing That Tried to Kill Me and the Love That Set Me Free

> **Journal entry: Long enough.**
>
> Being well and living whole is not something that I do, it's part of who I am. And that is enough x
>
> Who I am, is **enough**.

enough

> This pattern has gone on long enough, and I know that I want out, but this time I want out as far away as I can get from it so that I never go back in. The only way out is death. Death is the finish. Death means it's done. This death is not going to be my death, but the death of the thing that tried to kill me. I need to dig it out by the roots, poison it completely.

My intention for openly sharing my story is to offer people hope – not an empty hope that you can do whatever it is you put your mind to (expecting to work harder for the results) but hope that there is a way out, hope that there is a different way, hope that a life full of real love, real joy, real peace and real freedom is **possible**.

That is my prayer for my readers – that through sharing my story, I can shine a light on the way of hope I have encountered and lead you to also find hope in the darkness you may be facing, whatever that may be. After all, what is there to life without the hope that we can fully experience living the life we were purposed to live on this earth?

I've asked myself so many questions.

I've asked the Universe.

I've asked my family, friends, colleagues, mentors.

I've asked God.

Journal entry: Waiting for the new day

We don't have to wait for tomorrow's new day to start fresh.

It doesn't have to be a cycle of sleep it off and wake with renewed strength and a second chance.

It's not about how we put today behind us.

We don't have to suffer through all those waiting tactics.

The new day can begin right **now**, right here in this 12:09 pm hour. It's a new moment, and it's mine for the taking! The transformational power of recognising the present moment and the ability you have to choose will change your life.

If I pulled you up in your derailing of self-sabotage and pointed out the choices you had, would you still numbly, mindlessly choose the path of destruction? If you claimed to care for yourself and your future, no!

If you settled that you don't care and you're just going to go down the destructive path, then that's your call. Own it. Deal with it. The one you are robbing of freedom and abundance is you. Whenever you are consciously choosing that, you are agreeing that you don't want help. You're declaring that you'd prefer to stay in the stuck, sucky cycle you are in, and you agree to dealing with the pain it will cause.

Your call.

It's about awareness! You can become aware at any given moment in time.

For me, at my point of becoming aware, I would recognise and declare again 'I've had enough!'. I learned that at any given point, I could wash my face, reposition my ponytail, brush my teeth and stand tall in the identity I know is fuelled by love. Then, I could carry on in this new day, moment by moment. Forgiven and set free.

The greatness doesn't have to start tomorrow or wait until Monday for the new week. It's **now**.

When you choose now, you step–by–step figure out the how. You realise that all along, you didn't really need deep healing ceremonies, you didn't need trauma counselling, you didn't need to wait for that perfect moment sometime in the future when you're 'ready'. You realise that **now** is the **new**. And it's up to you.

N
O
W

N
E
W

Choosing now reveals how.

The Death of the Thing

Choosing new reveals you – you who are feeling stuck, abandoned, trapped, lost inside yourself. You are still there, deep down amongst the rubble. **You** never went anywhere. You just continued to make choices led by destructive thinking and feeling that held you hostage and took you off your destined path.

Now that you choose now, each moment there's new grace, new mercy.

You figure out how.

How might you honour your body right now?

How might you consider your dreams right now?

How might you love yourself a little more?

The new you (the real you that's been there all along) wants to experience fullness in this moment. You choose.

Now?

How?

New?

You?

I want you to read this slowly, and don't skip over it, please. It's easy to skip over it.

enough

Now becomes new.

There is no waiting.

There is no striving.

Step full into this very moment and take a moment to decide.

Do I want me to thrive in this moment?

Am I willing to surrender?

Yessssss!

Then receive the new moment because it's here. You can choose.

Here's what I say to the new me in the new moment that is now: Gorgeous, you've got this. Breathe in. There's grace. Breathe out, pressure is off.

No battle.

No pain.

Breath of life.

Peace that surpasses all understanding.

It's yours – right here, right now.

The Death of the Thing

There's nothing more to do.

There's nothing to make up for.

Nothing to be ashamed of.

You are human.

You made it this far.

There's plenty more testing that's waiting for you on the other side of this moment, but for now you are free, you are safe. You are enough.

Breathe in. Grace.

Breathe out. Pain. Torment. Past. Guilt. Shame. Ache. All of it! Gone.

Breathe in. More grace.

Breathe out. Doubt. Fear. Worry. Scorn. Scoffing. Gone!

Breathe in. Love.

Breathe out. Hate.

Breathe in. Peace.

Breathe out. Torment.

enough

Breathe in. Hope.

Breathe out. Despair.

Breathe in. Enough.

Breathe out. Enough.

Receive.

Now.

It's a new day.

It's a new you.

Go live it to the fullest.

Journal entry: 30 December 2023 – Wisdom extract.

In-the-moment cries for help. It's killing you. The more you succumb to this temptation, your soul dies a little more each time. Literally, this addiction, this thing, is **killing you**.

You're not meant to live this life to survive and just make it across the finish line at the end (whatever that looks like). You were born to thrive! And if you are not thriving but continuously struggling with these things that seem to be defeating you, you need to ask '**why?**'!

What is it that you are believing?

What is it that you are afraid of?

What are you trying to prove, hide or escape from?

It's not worth it. **Face up** to it. **Step up** to it. **Rise above** it.

Life is worth soooo much more than that quick fix of dopamine right now (although your survival instinct doesn't know that). **You** are worth so much more than that quick fix.

Recognise that the choice you make right now has the potential to either take you out or bring abundant life.

Choose accordingly.

Your life literally depends on it.

Making the decision early.

Pre–decide. Before the temptation is in front of you, decide in advance. Be intentional, understand and stay grounded in **who you are** – the new creation. You are someone who flees temptation and follows the way out before falling into its trap.

Decide first.

Then, go out and face the world on the offensive, not the defensive.

You can't fight from a place of victimhood all the time. You are a warrior, and you are victorious. It's essential to stride forward and embody that victory – claim it, own it and live it out. Establishing healthy boundaries will help you maintain your position and reduce the need to constantly fight and struggle.

For the Christian woman: I have several printable resources, featuring powerful scriptures, available for download on my website. Visit www.shereewrightauthor.com.au.

In-the-moment cries for help.

Journal what's going on. Literally stop what you are doing, get quiet, set a timer, listen to audio, pray, ask the hard questions, feel the feelings and journal what's happening for you. If that feels too unsettling, that's OK – just move your body. Engage in some exercise, pump up your favourite tunes and take a dance break. Remember, this is about finding what works for you and honouring your journey. There's no formula!

Once you've interrupted the pattern, take the time to work through what comes up. It's worth every inch of effort you put in. Trust me, your work can wait. Your kids can wait. Whatever it is you were doing that got interrupted by this destructive pattern of behaviour **once again** can wait – even if it's just a 30-second pause – and you can come back later to reflect.

The Death of the Thing

Your life depends on it. It's killing you.

I had to ensure that this thing – this addiction – was dying out with every moment it presented itself. Instead of feeding into it and allowing it to take over, my mission was to eradicate it so that it wouldn't poison the goodness and nourishment I was finally beginning to crave and experience. Each time I fought, my weapon was love.

CHAPTER 10

Confession: The Giant Leap to Healing

Awareness is the first step towards healing and finding freedom. Acknowledging where you are right now and owning **all** of it is key. We cannot leave anything in the shadows; everything must come into the light. If you are feeling like you can't do that with a trusted friend or mentor, at least do it with yourself. If you can be completely honest, raw and authentic with yourself – without guilt, shame or judgement – you will be able to step into freedom from any situation where you feel you are sliding into the dark.

It is so **powerful**. When I started to open up about my struggles and be honest before others, I had a few very close and

trustworthy friends that I could call on when I felt burdened by an attack or a temptation coming on. I would simply say 'I'm spiralling', 'I need prayer', 'I need truth' or 'I don't want to be alone right now; are you free?'.

These kinds of emergency texts immediately shone a light into my darkness so that I wasn't left in a place of torment and distress, which was sometimes so easy to fall back into if I wasn't looking after all of myself. Even if none of these people answered me or could be available right away, the fact that I took it out of the hidden parts of me and into the world by sharing honestly meant that a burden lifted immediately.

When I say looking after all of myself, I don't mean signing out of life and letting go of all of my responsibilities just to get a grip and refocus. I mean looking after myself in small ways amidst the chaos of the day or moment and honouring my needs – whether they be emotional, physical or mental. Taking a moment to pay attention to my breathing is looking after myself, getting myself out of my head and into my body. Drawing my attention to the things I am grateful for is looking after myself. Consciously being aware of what is going on right now, noticing my thoughts, acknowledging my feelings and being present and grateful will help **kill** my anxiety.

I ask myself what it is that I need right now and wait for a clear answer. If the answer is 'I don't know', then I would start with something – play music and let it penetrate my soul; move my body accordingly; lay down and do a 10-minute or 30-minute meditation (sometimes only a 3-minute meditation); grab a journal and write; grab a book and read; call a friend to check in on them and take focus away from myself for a moment; create something (a post for my blog or social media, a quote,

Confession: The Giant Leap to Healing

some Cricut designs, a nutritious wholefood snack); organise the linen cupboard, kids' wardrobes, office desk, computer filing, photos and screenshots on my phone; sit on the massage chair; lay or jump on the trampoline; do seven minutes on the SkiErg; go for a walk; pushbike ride with the kids.

There are too many to list here, but I suggest creating your own go-to list so that when you are stuck, you have a reference point and can at least start the shift when you very first notice where you are. Awareness and consciousness are everything. Pay attention.

This is all advice that I probably would have found available, but until I lived through it myself and realised what I really needed, there was nothing anyone could say or suggest that would have been helpful until I intentionally turned there myself and asked, 'But what is it for **me**?'.

It's wonderful having a bank of resources available like a bottomless pit, but until we know from personal experience what uniquely works for us, we are not going to be able to move forward in the leaps and bounds that we were designed to make.

I never really knew what worked for me because I was too afraid to try anything, fearing I would get it wrong and mess it up. Nothing ever felt right. If I couldn't make full progress on something or wasn't sure I'd get it perfect, I didn't want to start. I couldn't handle the pressure of making a mistake, so I just wouldn't try.

I've come to conclude, and I emphasise this point quite a lot, that there is **no** formula. Despite the abundance of resources

accessible to us via the internet, podcasts, programs, books and services – all of which are undoubtedly valuable – your story remains unique. **You** are unique and your path is distinct, and that's completely acceptable.

Confession, in my experience, is not the act of bringing forward your sins and dark things so you can be shamed and punished and held accountable. Confession serves as the floodway to grace that can wash over you once you have revealed all the hidden things. It is about bringing into the light the things you have kept in the shadows or darkness. It turns the light on and immediately eliminates the darkness. It's about being honest with yourself and with a God who knows **all** things anyway. Confession is about showing those things to a God who already knows but wants you to acknowledge them and understand that you are loved **anyway.**

I paid attention to the whisper reminding me that God knows more about me than I know about myself and yet He still loves me.

Do you grasp this concept? Regardless of your sin, shame, wrongdoing, guilt or anything else that lurks in the shadows, when you bring them into the light, they can be taken by the Savior of the world who sets you free. This realisation was so profound for me. Suddenly, I am not the one who has to carry the burden of getting myself out of this mess. A weight has been instantly lifted at the moment I surrender it all.

As long as you cling to those hidden things and try to conceal them, you will remain shackled in chains, unable to live up to your full potential. They **must go**!

Confession: The Giant Leap to Healing

The only path to true freedom is through confession. Confess all your imperfections, all your guilt and everything you feel hesitant to fully acknowledge. It's time to own them. The soul you are harming by keeping them hidden is your own. Remember, there is a Lord, King and Savior who hung on a cross, transcending time, taking on all the suffering they bring. If you don't have that same faith in God, I invite you to think about this.

The act of releasing your burdens, facing truth and accepting yourself fully can lead to profound freedom and peace. It is a fact of human nature that when we are not honest with ourselves or others, we create inner conflict and distress (I lived this for yeaarrrrrs). This lack of integrity fractures our sense of self and can lead to feelings of shame, anxiety and unworthiness (Who hasn't experienced some of those traits in their lifetime?)

True integrity requires us to be authentic, to align our actions with our values and to be transparent about our struggles and mistakes. I honestly think that my early childhood of perceiving and believing that I had to be perfect or else I was broken and no good laid the foundation for this condition to escalate, leading me further and further away from the truth, away from myself. I felt I had to hide all the bad parts about me.

Confession is a powerful tool in this process. It allows us to clear our conscience, mend our relationships and move forward without the weight of secrecy and deceit. When we confess, we take responsibility for our actions and open the door to healing and reconciliation. It's about being freed from the past and creating space for growth and transformation.

enough

Honesty and integrity are not just moral virtues; they are essential for our mental and emotional well-being. They foster trust, build deeper connections with others and empower us to live more fully and authentically. By embracing these principles, we can break free from the chains of our hidden burdens and step into a life of greater freedom, peace and fulfilment.

If anything is hidden in your life at the moment, you have an opportunity right now to be free from the weight of that.

Release.

Let it go.

Give it all.

Reveal it all.

Surrender completely.

Know that you are fully known, you are fully loved, and you have a purpose for being here. **Nothing in this world can change that.** Don't ever think that something you have done or part of who you are is out of reach of the healing love of God. **He knows!**

He wants you to fully heal, and He can only do that when you fully reveal all of the hidden things inside you.

So, confess, my friend. Find a quiet place where you can be alone with your thoughts. Settle in to the stillness of the moment and let it all out in the best way you know how. You might speak it, write it, draw it, paint it, sing it, cry it, imagine it – whatever

Confession: The Giant Leap to Healing

way feels most natural, do that. There's no need to overthink. Be completely honest with yourself. After all, your conscience already knows. Like a child, with chocolate on their cheek, owning up to sneaking the chocolate chips. By confessing, you can wash away the stain of any guilt, shame, bad feelings or wrongdoing and release anything attached to holding on to it, tied to the shadow.

There is a knowing deep within your heart that recognises the need for this release. It is crucial to your well-being. Perhaps you haven't realised it until now, or maybe you're on a journey of self-discovery – and that is beautiful too. It might not be something I say or do that inspires you but the next piece of your puzzle. Deep down you know what is right for you, so listen to that whisper. Tune in. Block out the lies.

Lies are loud, dominating and debilitating. The truth is a quiet whisper in your soul, and it will always set you free and bring peace.

Remember, even if you feel alone, you are not the only one who has ever struggled with these thoughts and feelings. Embrace honesty, let go of what burdens you and step into the fullness of your potential. The world needs **you** exactly as you were created to be.

You don't need to tell anyone your list if you don't feel comfortable doing so. This process is personal and for your own well-being. For me, it's always between me and the Creator of the World. No one can take that away from me.

> *Note: The eating disorder or addiction and embedded patterns are symptoms, not the original problem. You need to get to the root.*

enough

When you stop trying to fix and get rid of the symptoms and start digging out the roots (the problems), you can begin to fully heal, and your life can flourish again. There is no reason to continue the toxic patterns you are living. You have a choice. Every moment, you have a choice. Don't give that power away.

In confession, you are always received and welcomed with love and acceptance. This is the giant leap towards healing. No matter your actions or your efforts, you are still deeply loved. You are always loved whether you are behaving well or not. Stand firm in that knowledge. Truly know who you are at the core of your being, seek your purpose and unleash the abundant life available to you. Until you embrace that pure, unconditional love for yourself, you remain vulnerable to fear.

Be authentic. Your realness is where true transformation begins.

Secrets are darkness **where harm grows**. It's time to confess. Sometimes you will need to confess over and over again, and that's OK. I've been in that place where I've moved through a moment of weakness and thought I had conquered it, only to find myself helpless and hopeless at the mercy of temptation all over again.

Confess. Repeat as many times as necessary.

If you choose to deny the truth in that moment, remind yourself: 'Dear self, I messed up. I'm sorry. I don't mean to treat you like this. You definitely deserve better. I love you. I really, really love you.'

Confession: The Giant Leap to Healing

Before you judge me for writing letters to myself, check your own internal dialogue for a moment and listen to how you speak to yourself within your thoughts. Are they kind? Let's all be a little kinder.

Running for my life.

I continued with my running every morning as a foundational mental health plan – not extreme fast speeds or long distances, but daily self-care, fresh air, movement, increased heart rate and rush of endorphins.

Exercise really is the most underutilised antidepressant, and food is the most abused anxiety drug. I have lived and experienced this completely and am a huge advocate for doing things naturally to support mental, emotional and physical well-being.

I found that running first thing in the morning sets the foundation for me to have a better day – not always, but mostly. If I don't go for a run, I'm more susceptible to struggle, if challenged. I'm aware of that now, and I can strategise or intervene when I notice I'm at risk of going into a spiral. Often it comes back to lining up my body (physical) with my mind (thoughts) and my soul (emotions).

You don't have to copy my routine for morning runs. Everyone has their own thing that works for them. The beautiful part about sharing our strategies is that we now have countless options if we haven't found our own yet. We can tailor an approach that works specifically for us by gathering ideas and concepts from others and seeing which ones resonate. This process involves trying, failing and trying again until we **know** what works for us. This is the only way.

When I talk about finding your purpose, I don't mean it's something you have to search for out there in the world (as I used to think). I've come to realise it is more about remembering, returning and reconnecting with the original plan. This approach makes the journey so much more achievable and relaxing. Instead of searching the world for answers, turn quietly within and discover that it was there all along.

CHAPTER 11

What If It's Not About Me?

Why. So many whys. 'Why, God?!' I asked this many times and don't think I ever got an answer that didn't return to that whisper asking me, 'Will you let me love you?'

Turn and face yourself.

Silence all the voices. Listen to what God says about you. Every void demands to be filled. We get to choose – fill it up with truth, or let the lies creep in? Love or Hate? That hunger, that emptiness – fill and satisfy it with **good**.

enough

There will always be opportunities for us to numb the pain. But we have to realise that if all we ever do is numb the pain and not get to the root cause for healing, we will never deal with it and it will fester and get worse as time goes on.

Short accounts.

Keep short accounts. Feel it. Recognise it. Sit with it. Choose what to fill the space with. Be open to receiving love you may feel you **don't** deserve right now, because **grace** covers **all**.

There is enough grace and mercy to out–love any shortcoming or imperfection. We just have to be willing to believe and receive. And surrender. There's that **'let go'** concept again. When will I learn this one? When will I stop going around this mountain? That probably sounds very cliche and quirky. Girl, you just have to believe and receive, but I mean it. We get to choose what we believe. If we recognise a lie, it's up to us to quickly reconcile to the truth and be done with that lie immediately before it bears roots.

Ask yourself this: **Do you believe** that you can be **loved** in this situation, right where you are, as you are, without changing anything about you?

Now ask: Can you be loved in this situation? As in, are you **willing to receive** and **accept** that unconditional love?

I believe the answer is **yes**, absolutely, without a doubt. The love of God is all–powerful and all–knowing. Your freedom remains in the answer to the question 'Do you believe that you can be loved in this situation?'

What If It's Not About Me?

If you maybe–kind–of–sort–of believe a little bit, the next thing to ask is: 'Are you willing to receive that love poured out for you?'

Hold there for a moment.

I wish I could be sitting beside you, holding space for these questions to penetrate in your being because asking those two questions and finding out what's going on in your heart is going to be critical to how free you live your next moment. It's like receiving a gift – you must be willing to reach out and take it, accept and open it.

Stay with that, please.

Let's loop back again to those questions.

Can you be loved? Yes!

Do you believe that?

Are you willing to receive?

If not, **ask God** – however you would like to address a prayer – 'Heavenly Father, help me with my unbelief', and He will provide what you need in that moment.

I find it hard to articulate my heart in this place because if I had confided in someone about what I was going through (someone I know loved me), they would have looked me in the eyes and asked, 'Sheree, do you believe you can be loved in this moment, right now?'

That question would have cracked me open. The answer would have been a firm no. In that moment I would have realised that I didn't feel worthy, good enough or loveable. I would have admitted that I didn't feel like I was enough. That question would have exposed the lies. It would have forced me to confront the pain at its root and enter healing rather than just masking it, covering it up, numbing it and carrying on like everything was fine, like I was fine when I wasn't.

In my fear to face myself, I was digging myself deeper into the pit of despair, pretending it was all OK, when deep down I knew it **wasn't** OK. I wasn't OK. A few years ago, I came across a book titled Perfectly Hidden Depression by Margaret Robinson Rutherford, PhD. I heard the author being interviewed on Caroline Leaf's *Cleaning Up the Mental Mess* podcast. The book described my life with uncanny accuracy, leading me to a deeper realisation and understanding of what I have been experiencing. It was like another layer cracking open.

There comes a pivotal moment when we must ask ourselves quality questions. This moment isn't about waiting until we feel ready or reaching a certain stage in our journey – it's always now. Procrastination, resistance or avoidance won't make it disappear.

> **Quality Question:** What if the decisions or actions I'm afraid to make aren't solely about me?

> **Quality Question:** What if there's a grander purpose or broader impact beyond my comprehension?

What If It's Not About Me?

Quality Question: Who am I to withhold life-altering opportunities from others because of my own fears or reluctance to step out of my comfort zone?

Many of us struggle to recognise our own worth, which becomes the justification for holding back from significant life changes. We simply don't believe we are worth it. Yet, for those we deeply cherish, we'd willingly embrace hard things that lead to transformation.

Who in your life motivates you enough to do whatever it takes to pursue your dreams relentlessly?

Who would you literally lay down your life for?

Are you willing to forsake comfort and perfection to embrace the discomfort of growth and become the best version of yourself as you are destined to be in this life?

What would it take?

What sacrifices are you prepared to make? For me, it boils down to **focus** – where it lies, what demands my attention and where I must direct my energy to attain traction, momentum and breakthroughs.

The truth is that if we're feeling stuck and sense there's something more available but remain stagnant, we must ask ourselves: Who does it affect if I don't go searching deeper for this freedom?

Whether it's freedom from addiction or self-destructive patterns, financial freedom or the liberty to pursue endeavours that

nourish our souls, unapologetically embracing our authentic selves – flaws and all – undoubtedly requires courage and commitment.

I used to think my story would ultimately lead to a product – a prize answer that would solve everything, an unbelievable, groundbreaking solution to my problems that could help others and bring us financial abundance. I imagined building a business around this incredible, problem-solving range of products, believing it would provide the financial support we needed and bring security to our family, giving me the peace I craved and strived for.

Little did I know that my story offered far more than any product or well-paying compensation plan. My story offers hope, a shining light to the way of true freedom. And you can't put a price on that. No one can pay me enough to experience the breaking of chains and winning victory that comes with true freedom. That kind of freedom is priceless.

I had to reach a place of surrender where I could let go of the outcome, trust that the inner work was worth more than any sales pitch and focus on aligning my heart before striving for successes that left me flailing. I continue to work on this. It's continuous surrender, and that is enough.

So, I will stand over here and occupy my little space of the world, and I will leave a footprint using this word: *Enough*.

Journal Entry: Friday, 22 April 2022

There is a God-shaped hole in your heart from when you are conceived. Nothing in this world will fill it or satisfy the emptiness other than God himself.

When you put your trust in Jesus Christ as your Lord and Saviour and have faith that He is who the Word of God says He is, only then can you be set free and live with a whole heart.

When you are empty or hungry or unsatisfied, pause for a moment and allow yourself you be filled by God's unconditional love. Take a moment to really receive His love for you. Acknowledge His unconditional love and power in your life. Notice the difference in the way you feel, and notice the disintegration of the desire you just had for that vice – the addiction, the habit, the ungodly and unhelpful 'thing'.

For me, it's food. Now, I wouldn't say food is ungodly or bad (some foods are bad for us, but we take our common-sense approach in knowing about nutrition and how our bodies work), what I'm referring to here (and some people might know what I'm talking about or be able to relate) is my burning desire for a food when I'm not actually hungry. It's just a craving. Sometimes it could even be a good craving, and I snack on healthy food. But the ungodly aspect of it is that I use food as my vice. It's my drug, my comfort blanket. It's my obsession and addiction that has the power to kill me by means of a slow and painful death, crushing my spirit and moving me away from God and my potential. There, it becomes the ungodly thing.

Yours might be alcohol or something on the internet or procrastination away from what you know you're meant to be doing.

I'm no expert on these things. I am mostly experienced in the food battle. The procrastination can add a layer to my complexity and struggles; I'm saying I'm no expert, but whatever it is for you, I believe it's a similar concept.

Until you pause and allow the perfect love of God to fill your heart, you will keep struggling and fumbling and falling and making the same mistakes. It's not really us who have the power to change. It's God working **in** us and **through** us, so the (best) next thing we can do is surrender to God and allow **Him** to change our habits and our future. He's way more capable anyway!

Invite Him into the moment.

We are not the gardener here who has to pull out all the weeds, choking out the growth of flowers; **we are the soil**.

God is the gardener. Invite Him. Ask Him, receive His offering of help, of love. Give Him permission to remove these weeds from your life in every moment so that your soul (soil!) may be rich and fruitful.

It can be painful removing weeds. Be OK with that. It's necessary. Accept whatever will be and however God will choose to work. He knows best.

You've tried.

God knows you've tried **all** these years and all these times to overcome and rise up and conquer. And yet, you're still here.

It's OK.

It's time to surrender. Acknowledge God. Let Him into your heart **over and over again** until the healing is more than the problem. Then, you will know you are on your way to a greater life, and He can lead you to the path that you were meant to take. He has good plans for you, amazing plans. You just need to accept and receive. Be still. And know.

He is not giving up on you.

Journal Entry: Wednesday, 21 December 2022

Fear.

When you're in a state of fear (survival state), there's no room for connection, life or truth. You see others as a threat rather than support. You don't feel worthy of love.

enough

When we feel safe, we're able to let our guard down.

By holding back from the truth, you prevent your own healing. The truth can set you free. Truth propels us towards growth. Love and honesty are one and the same.

There is no fear in love. Perfect love casts out fear.

The truth doesn't need to be justified. The truth simply is.

The only way to eliminate shame is to bring it into the light and see it for what it really is. Keeping shame in the darkness will torment you.

I had been ignoring myself, lost from self, integrity.

Truth reaches out again and again **reminding** you to come back to the path. To align yourself with truth is always to move in the right direction. It hurts far less to feel the pain momentarily than to experience a lifetime of dishonesty and regret. It's not too late.

Communicating – I want, I need, I feel.

Afraid to vocalise out of fear of changing your mind, what if I get it wrong? People like me aren't in tune with their own wants, needs and feelings.

To be fully responsible for yourself is empowering. To always be empowered, always see love reflected back to you.

You are responsible.

You have the ability to respond to your circumstances.

When we react to life, we become powerless, losing our control.

Reflect on the last three times you blamed someone. Know what sort of dynamic was created for blaming instead of taking responsibility.

The insecurity and self-hate will fade away when you embrace all that you are without judgement.

Simply being loved, not fighting for it or striving for it.

What do you truly want?!

In the process, you'll be confronted by the parts of yourself that don't believe having what you want is truly possible. These are your perceived limitations.

Believing something is possible is the first step to being able to reach it. Desire is the easiest way to identify what you truly want.

Delight in the Lord. He will give you the desires of your heart. Desire is Holy. The Holy Spirit knows the direction you need to travel in order to connect to your Creator in order to expand. To resist is to deny yourself connection.

enough

Honour what you are drawn towards. Desire is our heart speaking to us.

Listen. Heal.

Suffering with mental health is one of those unknown navigations that looks completely different for **everyone**. There are no two experiences that are the same, because there are no two humans that are the same.

The thing with a cancer diagnosis or evidence-based health issue is that you can scientifically and medically track what's going on. You can search and find real data that tells a story. There are tests and counts and reports and all sorts of things to help the doctors gain an understanding of the illness and how to treat it. Humans are amazing. We've developed so much wisdom and advancement in the last 100 years. But (there's always a but) the thing with mental health is that there's no way to know the full depth of what is happening in a person's mind. The brain, yes, but the mind – that's a whole different realm. Thought patterns and beliefs express activity in the brain, although the torment and feeling inside the human soul cannot be measured. That is a very scary place to be if it's toxic.

I remember being completely in despair, so low I couldn't think even one thankful thought or delightful experience that would convince me my life was not a mess. The magnifying glass in my mind on the mess I was in and the pain I was experiencing was causing so much confusion.

> Real severe emotional pain can be much worse than some kinds of physical pain. If you've got something going on in your body, you can go ahead and get some medicine for it. When it's in your soul, God is the **only** one that can take care of it.

What the enemy meant for evil, God can use for good. No matter how dark or difficult your struggles may seem, they can be transformed into a source of strength and growth. I believe this perspective brings hope and purpose to even the most challenging circumstances – if you let it.

This is based on the biblical principle found in Genesis 50:20, where Joseph says to his brothers, 'You intended to harm me, but God intended it for good to accomplish what is now being done, the saving of many lives.'

In seeing my struggles and how this experience has shaped my life, I can choose to draw good from it. My encouragement to others struggling can be good. My awareness of how my body responds to certain foods can be good, as I intentionally fuel and nourish my body out of love and respect now and for the rest of my life. It's easy to see that there are many years wasted and many opportunities lost, but knowing that I can draw good from each experience means I have the freedom in this moment to be at peace and not play the victim.

When this becomes not about me but about helping others, shining a light and leaving a legacy, it transforms my journey into something meaningful and impactful. By sharing my story, I hope to inspire others to find this kind of strength and purpose, turning their struggles into stepping stones towards a brighter future.

What is it in your life that has felt like it has tried to take you out? How can you transform that pain into a source of strength? Take a moment to reflect on the challenges you've faced and consider how they have shaped you. Use that insight to fuel your growth and resilience. Remember, the same experiences that sought to break you can become the foundation for your greatest achievements and the inspiration you offer to others.

My passion is health and wellness and knowing your true identity full of worth and value. I never would have reached this level of understanding if I hadn't gone through my own struggles and journey of self–discovery. Each challenge taught me valuable lessons and brought me closer to the truth of who I am and the importance of nurturing the whole being – mind, body and soul.

CHAPTER 12

Are You Willing to Fight?

> **Journal Entry**
>
> The war. Battle. Internal fight. Default destruction.
>
> It's easy to resist when my flesh and willpower is willing to resist. But when I am weakened, I crumble. I feel myself failing, slipping away, unable to fight, unable to defend, unwilling to defeat. I fall victim and place pity upon myself with no consideration for the great power of God I have access to in my next breath.

enough

In these times, my focus is not on Jesus but on myself. I feel so selfish, so self-centred, self-focused. I am being so selfish, gratifying the desires of my flesh. Again. The ones I promised I wouldn't fall into temptation to again.

I cannot do this alone. There is power in surrender – not a giving up but a letting go. Stop trying in your own strength. Stop trying to fight. Stop trying to resist. Stop trying to apply your good works and dig yourself out of the rubble.

'Be still and know that I am God.'

Be still.

STOP.

Surrender your control to God.

Trust that He will take better care of you than you could yourself.

Obey His next instruction. You need to be still and quiet enough to receive what He is whispering to you in the storm.

Pray until you experience peace. Be still. Peace. Be still.

Jesus commands peace to the storm, and the waters become still. The wind and waves stop.

Are You Willing to Fight?

Breathe in his peace.

Until you actually stop in the moment, you will never be able to overcome this temptation.

Know that for every temptation, he provides a way out. This is it. Stop.

STOP – Surrender, Trust, Obey, Pray.

You must be firm, like a warrior fighting. Stand your ground. Be bold. Courageous. Get loud at the torment. Shout at the enemy. STOP!

Pray. Cry out to God. Let your heart guards down and soften to His gentleness towards you. Pray until you experience peace. Pray with thanksgiving. Let your requests be made known to God, and the peace of God, which transcends all understanding will guard your hearts and your minds in Christ Jesus. (Philippians 4:6–7)

Lay your burden down.

This burden of mine it's not self-inflicted. It's not something I chose. I didn't pull this upon myself. It was placed upon me, and I chose to carry it.

I continued to walk with it, to walk in it. To struggle. To stumble.

I surrender all. I let my body go with everything that I am. I let go and let God. This moment, there is a healing. It is not something I have accomplished on my own or achieved in my own strength or power. I have nothing. **I am** nothing, yet in Him I am enough. In Him I have everything. He is everything.

Listen to the words in the song 'Do It Again' by Elevation Worship.

To summarise, the battle is **won**. God has never failed me yet. His Word and promise will come to pass. He is still enough. He's faithful. I can remain **in** his love.

God has given us free will. Remember, it's still always our choice. He offers a way out. He's not going to be the one there stopping you like a robot controller. It's up to you to say no to the temptation and turn your attention to God's presence in your life. It's up to you to decide whether you will commit to the healing he has offered you and receive His promise.

You say you want this full life. I believe you. But do you really want it that bad that you will do the hard stuff and press on and fight and draw strength when you are weak? If you don't, that is when the enemy will use you as a puppet. That is when all your effort and application come undone, and you end back where you started – with a tangled mess, like a knotted ball of wool, leaving you feeling helpless, hopeless and unloved.

Are You Willing to Fight?

He said his promises.

He meant his words.

He declared his purpose and destiny and plan for your life.

You, in your actions, (and inability to stand and fight or surrender and let Him fight for you) declined his offer. Actions speak louder than words.

Next time you are faced with the temptation or craving or feeling of weakness, ask yourself these questions:

Do I **really** want what God has for me?

Do I **really** want to live this **full life** He has waiting for me?

Do I **really** want healing?

YES!

The answer is yes.

Stop **giving in** to the enemy and stand in your position of authority to claim it! This is where the breakthrough takes place.

It's not up to you to be strong. Receive God's power. Draw on **His** strength. When you are weak, He is strong.

enough

2 Corinthians 12:9 (ESV) – "'My grace is sufficient for you, for my power is made perfect in weakness.' Therefore, I will boast all the more gladly of my weaknesses, so that the power of Christ may rest upon me.'

We can't change ourselves at a soul level no matter how hard we try. True growth and transformation are only possible when we declare the truth of our weakness, stop living in our own strength and receive the power of a loving, present God.

Make room for the Holy Spirit to fill you, empower you and set you free, not because we are deserving of His help but because He loves us.

God knows human perfection is unattainable. He wants honesty. He values humility. He already loves you through Jesus's perfection.

Let that be enough and choose right now to receive His affections for you.

The difference between striving and surrender.

I'm not much of a fighter. I'm not super competitive, with a winning–at–all–costs attitude. I'm kind of like 'Oh, well, if I reach the finish line that's good, but if I don't, it wasn't meant to be'.

Are You Willing to Fight?

This has served me, but it has also stolen from me.

Let me put it this way: I've been the kind of person that when things get hard, I don't strengthen my fight and push on. I retreat back and shrink in accordance with my current ability. I stay comfortable, and I'm relatively happy with that (Well, I've been willing to put up with the pain it creates more than the pain to push through and have breakthrough). So basically, I am really good at doing the things I'm really good at, and I will push through and push on and strive to reach the point that I can reach. Nothing more.

In a fixed mindset state, once I start to stretch beyond what I know or what I'm already skilled at or can do well, I put the brakes on. I hold myself back because I'm not willing to fight the fight. I'm not willing to grow because of the pain.

This sucks! When you look at it like that and spell it out, it's actually a really defeating attitude to have, and when I realised this, I was horrified.

So, what can I do now that I'm aware? I know what it is that I want, and I know I am worthy of experiencing it. I can stand up and face the pain required to change. From experience, I've learned that the pain of staying the same is far more damaging than the pain of pushing through the next comfort zone or barrier that keeps us from our abundant life.

- **Rewiring the brain for success**
- **Renewing the mind**
- **Changing your mindset**

enough

These are all terms I've heard countless times and dismissed, thinking I already know this. It's not new; I've heard it over and over again – change your thoughts, change your life. Then the steps that happen in between that – changing your thoughts will change your feelings, which will change your behaviours, and that will change your life.

What I didn't realise was that I was missing a key part: the **feeling**. For so long, I remained a victim to my feelings because of my ignorance and 'stinking thinking'. There are deeply embedded thought patterns that make up all of us, running in the background of our minds. If we don't consciously choose (make a firm head, heart and body decision), then we will continue running those thoughts that create our feelings, actions and quality of life.

Have you ever noticed how there are extreme situations that people go through, yet their attitude and life reflect the complete opposite of what you would expect them to be feeling or living? I have observed this, and I've resolved that my struggle was not something I had to remain a victim to.

My struggle was a result of my deeply rooted thought patterns and beliefs. No matter how many good thoughts and lovely beliefs I layered on over the top, those underlying thoughts were still running my operating system. So, while I was in a richly loving relationship, I wasn't fully receiving the love poured out to me, leading to self-sabotage. And even when I encountered the inexplicable love of God upon discovering my personal faith, my head (mind) was still not fully convinced. My heart was in it, but my head resisted due to these old limiting beliefs – wiring, mindset, thought patterns, whatever you want to call it. I wanted to believe it was true for me, but deep down in my subconscious, I was resisting. This is not uncommon.

Are You Willing to Fight?

There is enough information now to help us understand how the mind works, and I am so fascinated by it, especially because I've struggled with it and could never figure out why. Additionally, the science confirms what's written in the Bible, and the Bible confirms the science. For me, aligning my faith with my head, heart and body was the threefold cord I was missing and needed to grab hold of in order to live a truly full and free life.

If you are saved and have Jesus in your heart, but your mind is a mess, then your life choices (being run by your default thinking patterns) are going to create outcomes that reflect that – a mess. That's why I struggled for so long. That's why the temptation remained strong, why the battle kept raging and why my soul grew weary – because I wasn't in full alignment in all those areas of my being.

The world now presents this concept as holistic living – being connected to the universe, nature and the god-self. All of that is lovely and works, but it's a temporary world fix to an eternal problem. We're not meant to live on earth forever. Our home is in heaven. There is no discrimination or exclusivity to get there other than answering 'Do you believe in my Son, whom I sent to die for the sins of the world?' (now I've paraphrased that), but basically, God – the Creator of the Universe, nature and humans – also created heaven, and that is where we are to live forever. Whatever striving we participate in to get us into heaven will count for nothing if we don't believe the truth. There is only one truth.

There is no grey area. It's black or white. Light or darkness.

The question is: 'Do you believe?' The answer is either yes or no. There's no 'Well, kind of, sort of. I believe this bit but not that bit, and where it says to do this in the Bible, I don't agree with that.' NO!

It can be this simple!

Yes or no?

If the answer is yes, then go and live like that! Enter into the love of God that He wants to pour out on you, and watch your life transform. If the answer is no, then first ask yourself why. Whatever answer or reasoning you come up with, also ask, 'What **do** I believe?'.

I hope that your heart is softened and your mind is open to the possibilities of God's love because He **is** the only way. There's a battle raging for your soul, and you get to choose whose side you're on.

I knew that God loved me (I know that God loves me), but when it came to fighting for my soul amidst these repeated challenges, I often felt overwhelmed. It's crucial to understand that we can't simply shrink back and become victims of our circumstances. Instead, I learned that I had to stand firm, drawing strength from God's love and promises.

This fight isn't just about surviving; it's about actively choosing to live in the fullness and freedom that God offers us, despite the obstacles we face. We are called to be warriors, not just survivors, equipped with faith and resilience to overcome every battle.

Are You Willing to Fight?

The final FU

Whenever I remained stuck in shame and guilt over my mistakes and not reaching the 'perfect' standard I had set for myself, I stayed trapped in the cycle of temptation, weakness and frustration, falling down, getting back up, falling down, getting back up, falling down again. Each time I'd get back up, I carried a little extra weight of shame and guilt. Shame and guilt that would hinder my ability to walk free and live light in the springy, excited stride I was born to walk. Heavy–burdened and a victim to my habitual behaviour, I felt like a victim – wounded and trying to hold all the pieces together without any real healing taking place.

This is torture. At what point does it become the final fall? The thought that if I fall and stay down and remain there, I'm a quitter. I've given up.

It's life and death. Giving up is not an option. Still, how can I fight any longer? I'm wounded. Heavy–burdened. Weighed down by the shame and guilt and pain of going there again and again.

I can't escape myself. I keep doing the same things. I keep falling into the trap.

The final FU is not what you might think. It stands for **Forgiven Unconditionally** – the declaration over my life. It's the stand against the plans of the enemy, affirming that I **am** forgiven. It's **not** conditional, and I am fighting from a place of victory. I am already free. This war has been won.

The moment I decided in both my head and heart that I was **not** a victim, I realised I did **not** need to carry the weight of my guilt and shame any longer. The moment I owned and accepted my imperfections and turned repentantly towards God and His offer of love, I could rest from the fighting. When I fully accept, I am **no longer** a slave to my weakness. Then and only then can I receive forgiveness and freedom that is offered to me – not the tainted forgiveness I offered myself, which had conditions attached, like 'as long as this is the **last** time, the absolute final time you do that, you are forgiven and released of all the others. But, that one had to be the last.'

What I needed was unconditional forgiveness. Forgiveness that says, 'Even if you stumble and fall again, it's OK; I will lift you up. I will be here. Grace will cover you. I will give you the strength you need. You don't have to carry this burden on your own. Lay it down, let it go. It's done. You're free! Go live like you're free and watch the guilt and shame wash away in my love.'

You are forgiven unconditionally.

When I grasped the full idea that Jesus's forgiveness never runs out, it was not permission to keep on deliberately failing or falling. It was permission to not have to be perfect and get it right all the time. So, when I did try (in my own strength) and still happened to fall down, at least I knew I'd given it all of my human effort, and Jesus is there to cover the shortcomings. **He knows** we are human and are set to fall prey to our flesh.

What a relief – like an instant aha that **I don't have to do it all. I don't have to know it all. I don't have to get it perfectly right.**

Are You Willing to Fight?

I am forever **forgiven unconditionally**. That is true freedom.

John 8:36 (NIV) 'So if the Son sets you free, you will be free indeed.'

Deeds are our works, our efforts, our own application to life.

We are free! We have freedom not to get it all right every time and that is so liberating. Once I removed that label from myself that said, 'She has to get it right every time or she's not enough', I was free. Free from guilt and shame and burden. Forever. Unconditionally!

CHAPTER 13

When the Mountain Doesn't Move

My struggle lasted so long because I never really went to war. I never consciously drew that line in the sand and said, 'Enough.'

Until I did.

This time, I am stepping into a new life and not crossing back over that line. This is my promised land, my new beginning. I claim it with all the strength and conviction I have.

Today, there's a battle line. I'm determined to stand firm in my authority. All this time, I've relied on my own ability to

enough

stay strong and overcome this struggle. But it's been useless, often getting me into an even bigger mess than before.

When I place my head in my hands, trying to fight what I face, I see the word *Enough* scribed on my wrist. It's usually my left hand pressing on my forehead, elbow on the table, eyes closed, head down, drawing deep breaths. As I open my eyes, the letters on my wrist are blurred. As my vision cross-eyes and I'm trying to focus, all I can see is a blurred, shadowy cross.

I know what word is written within it, but I don't need to be able to read it. The cross is enough to remind me where my freedom is. This symbol reminds me where I should focus when these moments torment me when my vision is blurred. Until I do this repeatedly in every changing situation, I will continue to face similar trials.

It's like a passing of the test. Confirmed – I'm strong enough and I stood firm enough to face this one. Then, I move slightly up that mountain, gradually working my way around and up, around and still up, until finally I reach the peak.

Yes, the Lord can speak to this mountain, and it will move.

But what if the view from the top is the glory I need to experience to fully grasp and understand that it was all worth it? Every single struggle eliminated in the moment of that mountaintop experience. What if climbing this mountain is part of the plans that God has for me?

When we come to accept what we face – to be what it is and stop trying to change the outcome – we know a deeper trust, a rest that cannot come through the path being paved easy or the mountain being moved. We know a rest that assures us of His unfailing goodness.

Moving the mountain takes away the muscle conditioning, fitness and strength that I would achieve by walking the road. Moving the mountain takes away the glory experience of being on top of the mountain and looking at the views of all that is around us.

From the top of the mountain, I am closer to Heaven than if I had still been ground level and seeing Jesus toss mountains into the sea.

Truth is that He **can** move the mountain, but He doesn't have to. Maybe he's not going to, and maybe that's OK. Maybe I'm OK with that.

Jesus wants us to walk some mountains, but he doesn't want us to walk alone. He is with us all the way, encouraging, strengthening, cheering so that we may make it and know the victory that is true victory.

The line I drew turned out to be at the base of that mountain. I crossed the line, then began the mountain climb that I promised I wouldn't back down from. I promised I wouldn't go back. This mountain is not one of those two-hour hikes; this could take a season. I'm prepared to face storms, wind, rain, turmoil, but I can take shelter. The Bible tells me this and now I understand.

- Cleft of the rock
- Refuge

enough

- Hide in the shadow
- Peace in the storm

Jesus, the Prince of Peace, is with me. With full surrender to the Son of God, anything is possible. This is the foundation of our faith.

Conquer that mountain, beautiful one. I can't promise it will be easy, but I know it will be worth it. There is never a situation too difficult or too hard when you open your heart to love.

The victory is yours. Stand tall. Stretch out your arms and declare '**Enough!**'

Afterword

As I close this chapter of my journey, I hope that you feel the same invitation I did – the call to stand in the freedom already won for you. This journey is not just mine, it's one we all must take. I believe in the victory that awaits you.

It's 2024, and I am 40 years old. Even as I write these words, I continue to fight battles within. But this journey has taught me that we never truly 'arrive'. We are constantly healing, constantly growing. We are a continuous work in progress, and as long as we have breath, we **can** make a difference – whether it's in our homes, communities, workplaces or even in our struggles.

I've learned that we are not defined by our past, our mistakes or the battles we've fought. We are defined by the love that is available to set us free. Stand in it. Claim it. Walk in it.

When temptation tries to pull you back, remember: You are forgiven unconditionally. You are victorious. You are enough.

Waiting so long to begin this process of publishing my book showed me that I was still chasing perfection.

I know that I don't know it all. I know that I don't have it all together. But I also know that, regardless of those facts, I'm enough. What I do is enough. What I have is enough. Who I am is enough.

My prayer for you is that you step into this truth and live in the light and peace of it every day. There is no substitute. The journey is worth it because every life is worth it. And the purpose God has placed within you depends on your decision right now, in this very moment – not in the past or the future but in the powerful present where real change begins.

About The Author

Sheree Wright is a devoted follower of Jesus, wife to a farmer, mother to three children, and a certified Results Coach through Authentic Education.

Her vision is to set up an organisation that supports mums in managing their daily lives at home. A beacon of encouragement in her various communities, Sheree is part of a network of women and mums who are building legacy income for their families through health and personal identity and connecting with others via social media to show how the extraordinary can be drawn from the everyday.

Living on a farming property just 10 minutes outside of Goondiwindi, Queensland, Sheree is dedicated to cultivating a simple lifestyle that fosters authentic growth and well-being. With a deep fascination for the interconnectedness of the mind, body and soul, she is passionate about health, wellness and living intentionally in alignment with her values. She delights in finding treasure at op shops and investing in wholesome, nourishing foods that fuel her from the inside out.

Follow Sheree on Instagram @successwithsheree or Facebook at Sheree N Wright to stay connected and be part of her journey.

enough

Speaker Bio

Sheree Wright is a farmer's wife and mother of three, with a passion for extracting the extraordinary from life's ordinary moments. Over the years, she has honed her personal and professional skills to break free from self-limiting behaviours and create a life of impact and inspiration, proving what's possible when you take action on your dreams from a place of love.

A former expert in procrastination, Sheree shares her wisdom, gained through quiet prayer and writing, to help shift perspectives and mindsets that keep people stuck. Her message is clear: We weren't born to live mundane lives, and it's okay to reach for more, even when feeling underqualified or not good enough.

Having a 'work hard at all costs' mentality left Sheree in a place of pushing a little too hard and not getting the results she was dreaming of, leading to a numbing that ultimately taught her how to feel again. Sharing ways that you, too, can feel and know within the depths of your soul what you were created for, is what lights the fire within that makes her unstoppable.

Sheree believes deeply in the power of authenticity, connection, and community. Her gentle but firm encouragement feels

enough

like advice from a trusted friend, creating a safe space for others to feel seen, understood, and filled with hope. With a strong foundation in biblical principles and whole health, she intertwines the genius of the brain, the magnificence of the body, and the extraordinary nature of the soul, urging us all to walk in our 'enoughness' and live purpose−driven lives.

If you're ready to embrace how enough you already are, invite Sheree to share her insights and life−giving perspective. She will leave you refreshed, inspired, and ready to step boldly into your true potential—one springy, excited step at a time.

Acknowledgements

I want to acknowledge the power and presence of God, who has gifted me with the ability to write and express myself through words. I receive many compliments on my writing style, and I cannot take the credit without giving all the glory to God.

I also want to acknowledge my husband, Chris. His love and friendship throughout my life have been beyond my expectations. I am honoured to do this life with him and raise our children together as a team. His steadfast commitment and staying power, especially through the trials and struggles I've faced, have been a true anchor for me. He's my best friend and one of the greatest remedies for my procrastination.

To all the friendships along the way – you know who you are. You call out the best in me and encourage me forward in my effort to walk in my 'enoughness'. You highlight the beauty of imperfection and grace that charges through all the negative self-talk and destructive inner critic.

enough

For this book specifically, I want to acknowledge my beautiful friends who convinced me that I could – and should – share my story. I am forever grateful. You are the ones leading the way and giving us all permission to try. You are amazing.

To my family of God, the church – both local (Goondiwindi Christian Church) and global (the many communities I have connected with online) – all of you who pray, who know how to shine the light in the darkness and continue to speak life into mine, I thank you.

Finally, to my family, the roots of where I came from – the past generations and future ones to come – I acknowledge that we're all in this together. No matter where the road leads you, there is always strength and hope in surrender, acceptance and shedding of more layers.

I love you. I love all of you. I acknowledge that I can't do this alone, and I am grateful I don't have to.

enough

Notes

enough

Notes

www.ingramcontent.com/pod-product-compliance
Lightning Source LLC
Chambersburg PA
CBHW061230070526
44584CB00030B/4066